T0285578

What's Your Dream?

Find your passion.
Love your work.
Build a richer life.

Simon Squibb

CROWN CURRENCY

NEW YORK

CROWN CURRENCY
An imprint of the Crown Publishing Group
A division of Penguin Random House LLC
currencybooks.com

Simultaneously published in Great Britain by Century, an imprint of Penguin Random House Ltd.

Library of Congress Cataloging-in-Publication Data has been applied for.

Hardcover ISBN 979-8-217-08644-3
Ebook ISBN 979-8-217-08657-3

Editor: Paul Whitlatch
Associate Editor: Amy Li
Production editor: Joyce Wong
Production manager: Heather Williamson
Publicist: Bree Martinez
Marketer: Rachel Rodriguez

Manufactured in the United States of America

9 8 7 6 5 4 3 2 1

First US Edition

To Aidan, my inspiration to make the world a better place

Contents

What's Your Dream?

Warning #1

When I meet people who say they are genuinely happy with their life, I leave them alone. I don't ask them if they have a dream, because I know they are already living it. I congratulate them and put my microphone away.

If that describes you, then put down this book. It's not for you. It won't help you and it might even do the opposite.

But if you have any doubts at all, any sense that there might be something else to life, or that you might want more, then read on. I wrote it for you. The people whose dream is still ahead of them. And especially those who don't even know they have one yet.

Introduction

"Unusual little lot, isn't it?"

It was my first time in a property auction room, but the man with the gavel was the one who sounded confused. He was about to open the bidding not on a house, an office, a block of flats, or a row of shops, but a staircase. Four stories high and four narrow windowpanes across, gray both inside and out, this building was an orphan. The block it once served had been redeveloped and now it just stood there, a literal staircase to nowhere, waiting to be demolished.

I'd heard about it the day before, half-listening to the radio while driving. "And there's a *staircase* for sale," the newsreader's voice had said in an upward lilt, eyebrows audibly raised. I heard the same tone in the auctioneer's voice the following day as I sat in the front row with my six-year-old son, Aidan, and my team, clutching a paddle and waiting to place my first bid.

Most people were treating this as a joke, but for me it was serious. The moment I had heard about this strange property being for sale, I knew I wanted it. As I drove, my mind went back thirty-five years. When I was fifteen, my dad had died suddenly. He had a heart attack right in front of me. In the weeks that followed, my mum and I kept clashing—two people going through pain, and two stubborn personalities who didn't know how to back down. After one particularly bad argument, she told me to get out and I took her at her word.

I

I think both of us thought the other was joking, but neither was willing to say sorry or seek peace. I left and never went back.

For a few weeks, before I found a room in a house that barely deserved to be called a squat, I had nowhere to sleep. There were a few nights crashing on friends' sofas and some spent outside. I would walk up the main street in St. Neots until I had left the town and then back again: anything to keep the winter cold away, anything to make the time pass. On one of these nights, long after darkness had fallen and when the quiet tells you that everyone with a bed to sleep in has gone to it, a crack of light caught my eye as I walked down the street. A door was ajar and I pushed at it. Inside, in the dim lighting, I could see the signs for a fire exit. I looked at the stairs in front of me and knew it was the best I could do: the closest I would find that night to shelter. Wrapping myself up in my big coat, I lay down and slept.

It was so long ago, but those words coming through the radio took me right back to that little sanctuary I had found. I knew that a staircase, even one that doesn't go anywhere, can have meaning. It can be the first step towards something much bigger.

The bidding started at $26,500. It felt absurd: all this money for a building that served no purpose. As a rule, I don't like buying property and even advise people not to invest in it. Yet here I was, being dragged into a bidding war for something that logic said was worthless. Up the price crept, from $28,000 to $30,000, at which point I first lifted my paddle. Still the bids were coming in from people not in the room: $30,500; $32,000. When I put my hand up again at $33,500, I wasn't sure how much higher it would go. But now that I had started climbing, I wasn't going to stop.

"Thirty-four thousand?"

The auctioneer asked the question twice but got no answer. The online bidders were done. The half-empty room was quiet. Then the gavel fell with a smart click. I lifted Aidan into the air and cheered.

"We got it!"

The nervous laughter that followed told me this wasn't how people usually behaved in the auction room. But this was no ordinary lot. Even the auctioneer admitted that he had never sold anything like this before. Almost immediately, I started getting calls from the BBC, the *New York Times* and others, asking why I had done this crazy thing.

Within minutes I had signed a contract and paid a deposit and was now irreversibly the owner of the strangest thing I will ever buy: probably the ugliest building in Twickenham. A taxi ride later, we were standing outside. A building with no address of its own, no post box, no real reason for existing. Gray and grubby, it sticks out from the back of a block of flats, with parked cars to the left and giant wheelie bins to the right. We didn't have the keys yet, but, like all those years earlier, the door was open. I pushed it and we went inside to a bizarre sight: all kinds of rubbish had been dumped there, including bicycles, bed frames, and fire extinguishers. It looked like an unsalvage-able mess. I immediately knew it was perfect.

The staircase was not just a trip down memory lane. It was about to become central to the business I had launched shortly before that trip to the auction room, one I believe will be the most important venture of my life. It's called HelpBnk and its mission is to help ten million people start a business and pursue their dream for free. The idea is incredibly simple: you sign up to the platform and either ask for help with your business or offer to help other people with theirs. I started it because, across more than three decades of being an entrepreneur, there were so many times I needed help or guidance but didn't get it, or couldn't afford to pay to access it. I've never forgotten what it was like to be fifteen, running my first business, and asking a local entrepreneur for help. He wanted money, and I didn't have it. I pleaded with him to help me anyway. And he smiled, shook his head, and said the words I have carried with me ever since. "If you don't pay, you don't pay attention." I've always known that isn't true, but it's taken me thirty-five years to prove him wrong. It's the reason I created HelpBnk: a platform that allows people to help other people, offering the advice, support, expertise, or mentorship that someone needs to pursue their dream. That's *my* dream: a world in which we all feel liberated to help each other for free and with no strings attached—giving without the expectation of anything in return.

For some time, I had been promoting this idea of #GiveWithoutTake as a one-man show, held together by my great team. If you know me for anything, it is probably as the guy on TikTok who approaches people on the street to ask if they have a dream, and sometimes offers them money to quit their job and pursue it. The more I did this, the more convinced I became that so many of us *already have* that dream. We just don't know how to go after it. We're afraid about taking the plunge, not confident in our ability, or unsure what the first step should be.

There are millions of dreams out there living in people's heads, waiting for the spark to light them. Ideas that have so much potential to change people's lives for the better. They just need a bit of help. One person to believe in them. I know that because when I approach people working in supermarkets, fast food joints, train stations, and building sites, so many of them can't wait to tell me, a complete stranger, about the brand they want to build, the countries they want to visit, and the difference they want to make in the world. About their dream to help people out of homelessness, support those suffering with cancer, or make clothes for people who have just been through traumatic surgery. That doesn't mean they hate their job, just that they believe there is something more they want to do with their lives.

All that potential is out there. Imagine what could happen if we unlocked it? I feel excited just writing about it, and that is why dreams are such a powerful force.

It's also how the staircase was about to find its purpose. Initially, I thought it might become a pop-up space where people could come to get advice—a shop floor for HelpBnk. Then Dudley, a member of my team, suggested an even better idea.

He pointed out another thing this building without a name, post box, or address didn't have. A doorbell. We could set up a doorbell with a video camera and invite people to come and pitch their dream. We'd record them all, put them up online, and find ways to help them. So far I had been approaching people at random, asking if they had a dream. Now, people who already knew their dream could come to the staircase and ring the doorbell.

And they did. The videos started flooding in: one person even tagged me in a post saying that they were setting out on a six-hour drive from Scotland to London to ring the doorbell. If I took you there now, to that funny-looking building off the main street in Twickenham, we would see something: a person standing there with a piece of paper, holding their dream in their hand, saying the words to themselves. We would watch them hesitate, do one last rehearsal, and then press the doorbell.

In this way, hundreds of people have come to the staircase

and taken that vital first step to achieving their dream—saying it out loud and telling someone that they are going to do it. We had turned this staircase to nowhere into the world's most unlikely dream factory.

I set up the doorbell because I believe one of the most important things you can do for a person is invite them to tell you their dream, take it seriously, and try to help them achieve it. I want to give people the help and encouragement that I desperately needed but couldn't get at fifteen, when I was homeless and penniless. I want more people to have the chance to achieve their dream, and to take the first step that will lead to many more.

This book is the next step in that process. It is my case for why everyone should be pressing the doorbell—even if that doorbell only exists in your mind—and a guide for what to do next. It is everything I have learned from starting, running, and investing in dozens of businesses through my career, and from talking to thousands of people at random about how to find and pursue their dreams.

In the book, I will look at why we need a dream in the first place, and how it can become a galvanizing force in our lives if we allow it to be. I'll talk about how to discover your own dream, which I promise you does exist if you know where and how to look. And I'll discuss what to do once you have it: the practical steps you can take to begin making a bold vision into a powerful reality.

I'll lean on my experience as an entrepreneur, from starting my first business aged fifteen and homeless in Cambridgeshire, to building Fluid, a digital creative agency in Hong Kong that was eventually sold to PricewaterhouseCoopers—something my wife, Helen, and I built from an idea on the back of a beer mat into a company that was acquired by one of the largest consulting firms in the world. I'll share lessons from the many entrepreneurs I have met along the way, some of them familiar names and others not. And I'll show how people who started with nothing more than an idea in their head have turned it into something incredible and life-changing.

My hope is that by the end of this book, your dream will no longer be a distant wish but instead a reality you can touch. By reading carefully, taking actions on the advice I give, and digging deep to find the purpose within you, this book can be a ticket to the life you have always dreamed of.

But first let me answer the questions I can sense some of you want to ask. Why does all this matter? Why am I making such a song and dance about dreams and doorbells? It's simple. When you have a dream, and when you have identified a purpose, it changes your life. Everything starts to make sense because you are no longer playing by someone else's rules. All the work you do is for a meaningful reason that makes it feel worthwhile. No more counting down the hours. No more having to force yourself out of bed in the mornings. No more working for the benefit of someone you will never meet. You have the only kind of motivation that matters—one you have instilled in yourself.

A dream is a powerful and necessary thing. It's also a serious business. We're not talking about woolly notions or idle daydreams here, but a rock-solid foundation: something you can build your entire life around. You need clarity in how you think about your dream, discipline in how you define it, and perseverance if you are going to achieve it. You have to escape the trap of aspirations that aren't real dreams, swerve the excuses and popular myths that stop us from pursuing our goals, and learn how to embrace fear, exercise your risk muscle, persevere through adversity, and pick the right time to quit and move on.

The good news is that all of this can be taught. These aren't special skills or magical powers. I have done it myself, many times over, and helped hundreds of others to do the same. To define and pursue a dream is not a luxury, but something that we all need and that every single one of us can achieve. Do it and you will never want to go back to life as it was.

Posing the question is just the beginning. It's what comes after that has the power to change everything. So I ask you: What's your dream? And do you want to know how to achieve it?

What's
Your
Dream?

PART ONE

Why Dream?

Dreams, purpose, and the things that get in their way

I.

The Myths About Life

For most of my life, I never thought about having a dream. I didn't know I needed one. In fact, I was past forty and had built and sold a company before the vital importance of it dawned on me.

Since I left home at fifteen and started my first business, doing basic gardening work, I had been on a treadmill: working all the hours each day brought, chasing every lead, coming up with new ideas. Now, after selling my business for millions, I could do anything I wanted. I had total freedom in my life for the first time. It didn't take long to realize that I hated it.

At first you don't notice what's missing. You spend some of the money you have made: a nice house, the car you've always wanted, the big vacations that had always been put off because of the business. You play golf, sit in a hot tub, and tell yourself that this is the life. For a while you believe it.

Then it hits you. Every person who ever said that money doesn't buy happiness: they were right. I'd always thought that sounded trite. Having started with nothing, I had worked and worked to the point where I had both plenty of money and the freedom it brings. I'd told myself that being financially secure and retiring at forty were what I wanted. Now I saw the truth: *making* money had fulfilled me but *having* it didn't. I was no longer building something but instead holding on to what I had.

Now that I had all the freedom in the world, and enough money never to work again, what *did* I want? Thinking about that made me realize that nobody had ever asked me this question. Even worse, I'd never asked myself. At school, the assumption had been that we would get a manual job and aspire to nothing more. Then, after I left home, I had no choice: I needed to find work and make money to survive. In different ways, I've been doing that ever since.

I had thought endlessly about how to make the businesses I ran successful. But I'd never once thought about what it meant for *me* to be successful. What a good life was. What would lead to happiness and fulfillment. My eyes had been trained on a single spot, and I'd been missing the rest of the picture.

The nudge came when I was fulfilling my one steady commitment: taking my son to and from nursery school. In search of a community, I had been experimenting with social media and posted a video after dropping him off one morning. I said what was on my mind—that it was the best part of my day and that, right now, I felt like the luckiest man alive. I was living a dream, no longer needing to work, and able to spend as much time as I wanted with my son. It felt like success.

At that point, I had a tiny audience of a few thousand followers. For whatever reason, the video went viral, the first of mine that had. Soon the comments started rolling in, something I wasn't then used to. Some were humorous ("I'm broke and I get to do that") but others were critical. One in particular caught my eye.

"Stop posting this shit. Not everyone gets to have a dream."

First the comment annoyed me, but soon it intrigued me. Why not? Why shouldn't anyone have a dream? In fact, shouldn't everyone?

Then it started gnawing away at me. Did I have a dream?

Had I ever? And was this it? Much as I loved looking after Aidan and helping to raise him, I knew it wouldn't last forever. Before too long he would be grown up and have a life of his own. He'd no longer need me. So, what was my dream, something I could spend the rest of my life pursuing?

I couldn't let the comment rest and, back at home, I tapped out a response. "Have you got a dream? What's your dream?"

What's your dream?

It's a deceptive question, one that seems simple but is actually difficult to answer, which appears innocent but is also deeply provocative. It can sound naive when asked, but your response will be incredibly revealing about where you stand in life.

That morning and that reply was the first time I ever asked the question. Some people get to say their parents inspired them, others a sibling, a teacher, or mentor. For me it was an internet troll. So thanks, random TikTok person. If you don't like what you are about to read, blame them.

I never did get a reply from that unhappy commenter. But their words stuck around in my mind. If I hadn't had a dream all this time, what had I been doing? How had I built my company to a successful exit, and had I done it in the right way?

It made me think, for the first time, about what success really is and how we can achieve it.

I thought about the companies I had built, the successes and the failures, the stories I had told myself then, and how I looked back on them now. In the process, I realized something. We have some *weird* ideas about what success is and how to achieve it. Myths and misconceptions that mean we often target the wrong things and pursue them in the wrong way. Stuff that gets in the way of a real dream.

When I reflected on my life with the benefit of hindsight, I saw that while I had succeeded by any objective measure, I had also gotten a huge amount wrong. I'd not just made mistakes, but had also misunderstood things. I'd been dazzled by myths and blinded to some more fundamental truths.

My journey towards understanding the importance of having a dream began with identifying these myths and the role they had played in my life. I believe yours should too. Just as a gardener prepares the soil before laying turf or a painter sands a wall before picking up their brush, you will need a clean surface to which your dream can stick: one free of the ideas most likely to undermine it.

This is important because these myths are everywhere and they are powerful. They begin with what we are often taught at school and they continue to be reinforced throughout our lives. The myths are so prevalent that it's easy to live a whole life according to them.

Before we properly engage with the idea of the dream, first we have to get all this baggage out of the way. We need to deprogram ourselves of some of the most common—and often most harmful—ideas that have been handed down to us. The ones we were told never to question (which explains why one of my mantras in life is that you should question everything—and that includes what I am telling you here). These myths will kill your dream unless you learn to identify, reject, and overcome them.

Myth #1: The harder I work, the luckier I get

The first myth is one I only figured out when looking back on my career. For fifteen years, I had told myself that the business was doing well because I and everyone else worked hard.

Because of long days, late nights, and the willingness to always make another phone call rather than giving up for the day. We've all heard it—the harder you work, the luckier you get. It makes sense, right?

And I *had* worked hard. Compared to the brilliant creative talents of my wife, Helen, who I'd built the business alongside, working hard was the only real skill I had. That had been the deal way back when we had the idea to launch a creative agency called Fluid soon after we had first met. She would do the design work and I would do the selling. In all the years that followed, as we built teams around us, it never really changed.

The hard work had been necessary, but it wasn't the reason we succeeded. On its own it didn't explain anything. I had been around long enough to know lots of people who had put their hearts and souls into projects that hit the rocks. I'd seen entrepreneurs burn out trying to make their businesses work, having not stopped or taken a vacation in years. When I really stopped to think about it, I knew that hard work has as much in common with failure as it does success.

But all that time we were building the business, I *hadn't* thought about it. I'd taken for granted that success came because we worked hard. That our growth was the product of elbow grease above all else. This view was reinforced by what people would tell me when we had successes. "Well done, you worked hard for that." As if effort was the only reason for what we had just achieved—not skill, judgment, creativity, or luck.

Why do we all get so seduced by this idea of hard work, and insist on using it to explain our achievements? Why is this myth so pervasive?

One reason is modesty. When people are asked what made them successful, many will credit it to others: they had good parents, good teachers, a great team. And if they are really pushed, they will cite hard work. Most of us find it a lot easier to say "I worked hard" and "I got lucky" than to say "yes, I did well" or "we were smarter than our competition." Hard work is a palatable explanation for success that means you don't have to admit to your own ability or make a big deal about what you did right. We say it, and hear it said, so often that we have come to believe it. That's what makes it such a common lie: people don't even realize they are telling one.

Still, false modesty alone doesn't explain this myth. We actively venerate hard work in its own right. It's one of the fundamental beliefs we are taught right from the beginning.

Think back to school. In the early years, it was fun. Painting, drawing, story time, singing, dancing, games. Then, at the grand old age of about seven or eight, it changed. We had to grow out of all these wonderful creative things. To scorn them as childish pursuits only fit for younger kids. Now we had to do it differently: memorization, examination, pass and fail. The more you could remember and repeat, the better you would do. We learned, for the first time in our lives, that success was about hard work. Work hard at school so you can get a good job. Work hard at the job so you can buy a house. Work hard to provide for your kids and buy a bigger house. Keep on working hard so you can retire with a good pension. Whatever you do, don't forget to work hard.

The problem with all this isn't that hard work is a bad thing. We all need to do it, and if we are following a dream, we will manage without trying.

The problem is making hard work the end goal. Saying that if you embrace it, then you are bound to succeed. Spreading the idea that it's working hard, rather than working on our dreams, that will bring fulfillment.

This mindset tells you that you don't have to think. That you should simply put your head down and get on with the task at hand. Work hard and the rest will look after itself.

It's part of a prescriptive view of life that says you should be sensible, realistic, and careful. *Don't* quit your job and start a business. *Don't* pursue a career that isn't reliable. *Don't* try things that the people around you can't understand or relate to.

That's why I have a problem with the gospel of hard work before all else. Why I think it's a dangerous myth. Because it tells us NOT to dream. Not to pursue our biggest ideas and deepest ambitions if there is an element of risk about it. Not to step off the treadmill and think about what we really want from life.

Instead, we are meant to carry on, walking the same path as our parents and peer group, toeing the line and trusting that our hard work (usually on someone else's behalf, and mostly for someone else's benefit) will be rewarded. And we are supposed to think of our dreams as a form of hard work that is *too* hard—unachievable, unrealistic, and even selfish.

It's a narrow, self-denying view of the world. And I know it to be a lie because, although I have worked plenty hard in my life, my greatest success came when I wasn't working "hardest." I had my best ideas for the business when on vacation and my mind was not thinking about the company. I made the most money in Fluid's final years when we brought someone else in to run the business and I took a backseat. And in every business I've run, results have improved as I learned to delegate important jobs to good people. The less I have clung to the myth that hard work equals success, the more I and my businesses have thrived.

There is a lesson here: we don't succeed by forcing ourselves to work hard as some kind of punishment. In fact, we achieve the most when we work *smart*, and when we are working on something we really want to do. When we are following a dream that lifts and propels us, rather than banging our heads against the door of hard work for its own sake. That's why the first step to success is to leave this myth in the school textbooks, where it belongs.

Myth #2: Failure means disaster

When I ask people if they have a dream, I always have a second question waiting. After someone tells me what their dream is, first I congratulate them. And then I ask them: why haven't you started doing it yet?

People give lots of reasons, and a little later we'll look at these barriers in detail and consider how to overcome them. But the one that really sticks in my mind comes via four words, usually said in a slightly softer voice than the ones that preceded them.

"It might not work."

Of all the myths that society and traditional education promote, this fear of failure is perhaps the most harmful. We are taught to believe that there is something wrong about getting it wrong. That failure is an embarrassment—a dirty secret to hide away. Proof that we are stupid and lacking in talent. That we will never be good enough. It is a pervasive and corrosive idea, one that encourages us to give up on our dreams before we've even tried.

Like the belief in hard work, this begins at school. Often, in the classroom, we are taught that there are right and wrong answers, or that we have to produce our answers in a particular way to get marks in an exam. That continues through getting those exam results and a university place or apprenticeship. A prestige job and then another one after that. Promotions and performance bonuses. These are all things we either succeed or fail at. You've got in or you haven't. You're above the line or below it. Success is heaven and failure is hell.

The problem with this belief is that it bears almost no relation to how people actually achieve things, and what it takes. Try finding a successful entrepreneur who doesn't have dozens of stories of failure: the businesses that went wrong, the ideas that came to nothing, and the decisions they lived to regret. Try finding an inventor without a list of failed prototypes as long as the dictionary. Try finding an actor who has never failed an audition or an athlete who has never been dropped from the team.

Consider Jamie Oliver. By anyone's standards, he is fantastically successful. He's one of the UK's best-selling authors of all time (behind only J. K. Rowling and Julia Donaldson, author of *The Gruffalo*). He's one of the biggest stars on TV. And he has made a huge impact on society through his campaigning work on healthy eating.

He also had one of the most catastrophic business failures of recent years. In 2019, his business empire collapsed. His company filed for bankruptcy and closed twenty-two restaurants, laying off 1,000 employees. Most painfully of all, he had to shutter the first restaurant he had opened, Fifteen, where all the staff members were young people from disadvantaged backgrounds or with troubled lives. For almost two decades, he had been changing the lives of everyone who worked in that restaurant (and its offshoots around the country). It was a brilliant business with a purpose to rehabilitate vulnerable young people, giving them a second chance and a career for life. Now he had to stop. In the process, he lost $33 million of his fortune trying and failing to prop up his restaurant group and avoid bankruptcy. "When it was all going wrong it felt like a colander: the business was full of holes and there was nothing we could do to plug them," he later said.

It was a huge failure, he was vilified in the press, and he wept on television when being interviewed about it. But that failure was also relative. It didn't diminish all the things he had already achieved. Nor did it stop him from making a comeback. By 2023, his businesses had returned to multimillion-dollar profit; he was opening restaurants again and expanding his cooking school. He vowed not to return to the oversaturated chain restaurant sector, nor to try and grow as quickly as he had before. He had learned from his failure and didn't let it stop him from succeeding. In fact, it seems that failure motivated him to carry on, to rebuild what he had lost, and to do it better the second time. I bet if you asked him, he would say he became a better entrepreneur because of the huge failure and financial loss he had endured.

That may be an extreme example, but it contains a universal lesson. While we might not all lose millions in a business failure, we *will* all experience failures that feel disastrous. We have to accept that and be ready for them. More than that, we should embrace these moments. Rather than accepting the myth that treats failure as something to avoid, we should see it as something we can turn to our advantage. We have to pursue our dreams in the full knowledge that we will fail along the way, and get better as a consequence, rather than letting the threat of failure stop us from ever trying at all.

Take it from someone who has seen plenty of ventures fail as well as a few succeed. You learn from every single experience and you get better *because* you failed. It makes you better equipped to succeed the next time. You become more aware of the pitfalls and less surprised by the events that seem unexpected at first, but which with experience become predictable. Through failure, you gather data and develop insights that you couldn't have gotten any other way. That is how you gain knowledge, hone your instincts, and ultimately achieve an ambitious dream.

One of my most significant failures was in an unlikely field— comic books. While running Fluid, I started a joint venture with a prominent entrepreneur in Hong Kong. We had plans to invest in all sorts of things, from concept restaurants to major sporting events in the city. Our first project was a graphic novel. At the time, the Marvel Cinematic Universe had just started to gain traction and superheroes were becoming big business. Our idea was simple: what if Batman had landed in China, or Superman had been born in India? What if we could do for the East what Marvel and DC had done for the West? The result was *DevaShard*, a comic book about two brothers that took its inspiration from the *Mahabharata*, a Sanskrit epic poem dating to the third century BCE. It was fresh, beautifully produced by a mix of local artists and industry names, and immediately attracted attention.

The feedback was overwhelmingly positive and it looked like we had a winner. Especially when we started getting interest from major production companies to turn our comic into a movie—which could have transformed it from a niche publication into a global hit. Twice we thought a deal had been struck. The second time, we signed a memorandum of understanding with a major movie production company, and the press reported that they were going to turn *DevaShard* into an $80 million movie on the scale of *The Lord of the Rings*.[1]

Excited and confident, I kept spending more on *DevaShard*, adding better production values and more talent for subsequent editions. But the movie business is slow and it's a place where assurances run far ahead of guarantees. Slowly it became clear that the headlines and memorandums were never going to amount to anything. By the time the second deal fell apart and we accepted that *DevaShard*'s movie dream was dead, we had spent $1.5 million. All that money had bought a beautiful product, loved by fans, but as a serious business it had no future. We were forced to eat the loss and shut it down.

It was a huge setback. Never before or since in business have I poured so much money down the drain. But since I got over my initial disappointment, I have never regretted doing it. Despite the financial losses, this was the most rewarding failure of my life. I had a great time learning about industries I knew nothing about, including traveling to San Diego to present *DevaShard* at Comic-Con. I still love the product that our brilliant team created and believe maybe one day its time will come. The experience also solidified some business lessons, most importantly not spending what you don't have and plowing money into a venture based on vague promises. I had learned so much that I didn't know before and was a better entrepreneur for the experience. A few years later, I also found another reason to be grateful for this failure. One of the producers who had wanted to make a movie out of *DevaShard* was Harvey Weinstein. He'd shown interest in the comic and wanted to build a movie around one of the characters. The terms didn't work for us and we walked away from the deal. When the business failed, that "no" started to feel extremely costly. I looked back on it as a missed opportunity and blamed myself. Much later, I realized we had probably had a lucky escape. It turned out "no" had been the right answer after all, and failure had been the right outcome. One of the most important lessons I can give you is that you don't want to be in business with the wrong people.

My experience with *DevaShard* helped to convince me that you must learn to get comfortable with failure. You have to embrace it, learn its lessons, and accept that failure is often the price of risk. Above all, you cannot let yourself be defeated by it.

That doesn't mean we can banish the fear of failure. It's normal and healthy to not want to mess up. But this is an impossible hope. If you are taking the right risks, often enough, then you *will* have big failures in your life. The important thing is how you respond to them. How well you can train your mind to live with failure and learn from it. The more comfortable you are with getting it wrong, the better you will become at taking risks that pay off—risks that are needed to achieve a dream.

Before you can seriously pursue your dream, you need to confront any fear of failure you may be feeling. My advice is to define the problem. Under that general sense of fear is a deeper, more specific feeling, which you need to identify. Do you fear going broke, being judged by others, being rejected, or having someone's negative view of you proven right? Name the fear, write it down, and try to understand its source.

Perhaps the fear is material: running out of money and not being able to provide for your family. That's a practical fear with a practical solution: you can get your costs down, build up a rainy day fund, and get to the point where you have some protection against failure before taking the plunge. Or your fear may be rooted in the idea of what other people will think. That's a psychological fear that you can train your mind to overcome. Remind yourself that people often judge and criticize others as a twisted form of respect. They wish they had the courage to do what you are trying, and by criticizing you they are deflecting from their own shortcomings. In those circumstances, your fear is simply a reflection of their own. Understand that, and it becomes much easier to set aside.

Never let other people define what it means for you to succeed or fail. Don't create an illusion of how you think others will react and allow this self-made prison to stop you from pursuing your dream.

When I am setting out on a major project or new business, I always ask myself the same question. Does the mission justify the risk? If I can satisfy myself that it does, then I know I can control my fears, and will accept any failure that results.

Myth #3: It's OK to avoid hard things

Our ancestors had to go out and hunt. It was hard but it gave them purpose—providing and fighting for the ones they loved. Now the world has changed and most of us buy our food from the supermarket rather than tracking it through the forest. Life has become immeasurably easier and we should be grateful for that. But we also need to recognize what we have lost—how no longer needing to fight daily for our survival has blunted our senses, dulled our appetite for risk, and made us shy away from doing what is difficult.

Today, we live in a world engineered for convenience and instant gratification. Buttons are tapped and things are delivered to our doorstep. You can work at home, have most things brought to your home, and in fact it's easier than ever just to stay at home when it's raining and you don't want to face the world.

All that is fine up to a point. Who doesn't love convenience? As someone who predominantly works through social media, I'm the last person to say we need to go back to the Stone Age.

But we should know where all this can lead us if we don't adjust for it. We must be alive to the dangers of how choice leads us to take the easy option, convenience becomes laziness, and comfort feeds a lack of ambition. All the technology at our fingertips is a wonderful tool if we use it well, but a corrosive influence if we don't. It can encourage us to be the worst version of ourselves and not the best.

The biggest risk of all this is that we start avoiding the things that are difficult—exactly the ones that we need to achieve any meaningful dream. Our modern way of living can feed the idea that hard things are too much effort when there is always an easier option to take.

If we accept this, we lose the very thing that makes us special. As humans we learn through experience and we grow through adversity. The hardest times of our lives are often the ones that really shape us. We don't want life to be hard all of the time, but we do *need* it to be hard some of the time. Without those knocks, we don't grow as people, develop the confidence that is born of resilience, or prepare ourselves to tackle the most important challenges of our life. What's more, the "hard things" are often so much more difficult in our minds than in reality. The longer we build these things up, the more intimidating the prospect of them becomes. Whereas if we force ourselves to tackle them, we usually discover that our fears were misplaced.

I was reminded of this when I met someone not long ago in Hong Kong. We were filming and it wasn't until I had stopped this guy and asked him about his dream that I realized I knew him. More than twenty years earlier he had worked for me. It hadn't gone well: at interview he had told me he was hungry to succeed, but within a month it was clear that this was not the case. It wasn't the right job for him at that point in his life, and he wasn't willing to do what it would take to succeed. Rather than dragging out the pain for both of us, I told him that we would be letting him go before the end of his probationary period. Now, over two decades later, he laughed and said that his dream was to work with me again. Because, although he had been financially successful, with a career in banking, he felt unfulfilled. He hadn't taken enough risks, but had hopped from job to job and, as it happened, marriage to marriage, having been divorced three times.

I don't think it is doing this person any disservice to say he had not achieved what he wanted because he kept chasing the easy life and ducking the difficult things. He'd avoided making life hard for himself, and was left feeling a little empty as a result.

There is a simple lesson here: whatever you want to achieve in life, whatever your dream may be, I promise it will be difficult. Staying the course—in a job, running your business, in a marriage or relationship—is hard. To do so you need to adapt, grow, and develop as a person. People who are willing to tackle hard things will do this, and those who prefer to sit on the couch and take the easy option generally won't.

That is why we need to break the myth that it's OK to avoid hard things and to want to make your life as easy as possible. Unless you are willing to make life hard for yourself at least some of the time, you won't grow, you won't progress, and you won't achieve your dream.

Here's my advice. Put this book down for a second and make a list. Call it "the hard things." You will know them already. There's a call you have been putting off making, a role you have been thinking about applying for, a side hustle or project you have been promising yourself you will get started with. Write them down and pick one to start right now. I guarantee you will feel better the moment you accomplish the first thing on your list. You will stop thinking of these things as "hard" (and therefore unapproachable) and start embracing them as necessary: things that will give you a better life, steps you are taking towards your dream.

That was the experience of one woman who told me her dream was to be rich. I said that sounded great but she would need to learn sales—the number one skill in life, and something we must all do whether it is in our job title or not. But she had never sold anything. For her, this essential skill was one of the hard things in life she thought she was better avoiding.

Before she could give me all the reasons why she wouldn't be good at it, I took a pen out of my pocket and offered her $100 if she could sell it to someone on the street in the next sixty seconds. There was no training, no pep talk, no planning. She just started approaching pedestrians and starting up conversations like a pro.

With thirty-three seconds to spare the deal was done, and I was delighted to hand over the $100. Later she DM'd me and said those twenty-seven seconds had changed her life. She felt confident now. All because she had been brave enough to do something she was afraid of. She'd tackled a "hard" thing, and now she knew she could do it again. My $100 was in safe hands. Having overcome the hurdle in her head, now she was ready to scale her life and attack her dream. She had learned the big secret that the hard things are often so much easier than we imagine. Which is exactly why we should run towards them and not away from them.

Myth #4: Possessions make you happy

Some of the dangerous myths about life concern what it takes to be successful. But one of the biggest ones is about what it *means* to be successful. This myth says that you should measure your success by your material possessions. The house you live in, the car you drive, the vacations you can afford to take. Enjoy the fruits of your hard work (and make sure everyone can see you doing it).

For a long time, I believed this. Although I have never been a particularly materialistic person, and always preferred to invest money back into my business than to spend it on nice things, there was always one possession I *had* wanted. One I'd thought about when I was homeless and scrabbling about to put money in my pocket. If you'd met me then and asked me what my dream was, I'd probably have said this. I wanted a Porsche. A nice, fancy, expensive car that would be a sign to myself and to the world that I'd made it. That I didn't have to worry about how much it cost, and that everyone would know I'd succeeded.

That's why we love possessions: they speak for themselves. People don't have to ask; they only need to look.

So, when I could finally afford the Porsche and justify buying it, after selling my company, I went and got it. Driving it out of the showroom in Mayfair for the first time felt *amazing*. It was a moment of genuine euphoria, not quite believing that I had once had literally nothing, and was now sitting in a car that showed I could have anything.

That feeling lasted for about a week. I talked about the Porsche constantly and took every excuse to drive myself and other people around in it. Then, in the second week, someone scratched it. I spent three days going back and forth to the garage to have this very small problem fixed. What would happen, I wondered, when something really went wrong?

By week three, I realized what this "dream" was really like. I was anxious driving the car, fearful about it getting damaged. I was bored hearing myself talk about it. I thought I owned this car, but actually it owned me. It was making me more worried than happy. If it takes a certain person to own something like this, then I clearly wasn't one of them. When I sold it, I couldn't have been happier.

I had learned an important lesson: **a possession should never be your dream**. In fact, it can't be. Let's take another common example. When I ask people what their dream is, often they say it's to own their own home. I get it, but let me tell you how it goes. You save up and get a mortgage, which traps you in your job. You move in and before too long it's not right anymore: you have children now and need more space. Wind on a few more years and you want a bigger garden, your kids need their own rooms, and you move again. You worry not about the life you're living but the kind of place you're living in. You're on a conveyer belt: saving for a deposit, the mortgage payments, the need for a bigger house, the home improvements. Before long, these things are owning you.

When I say this, people sometimes respond by asking: don't you know how expensive renting is? And I get that, but I have to tell you that rent vs. mortgage is the wrong way of thinking about this. A mortgage might be marginally cheaper in terms of monthly outgoings, but that hides the many costs of home ownership: the money you have to spend on maintenance when things go wrong, the opportunity cost of putting all your savings into a house deposit rather than a business that can make you money, and the mental space taken up by the house being your problem and not your landlord's. The reason I tell people to be wary about putting everything they own into buying a house is that it limits your options. Suddenly all your money and much of your time are focused on this one thing. Whereas without a mortgage, you have flexibility. If I'd already been a homeowner, I might never have moved to Hong Kong, where I saved money by sleeping for months on a friend's sofa, and my business career might never have taken off the way it did. That's why the real choice isn't mortgage vs. rent, but mortgage vs. freedom.

Here's something that may surprise you (it certainly surprised me). Every time I get rid of a possession, I feel freer. Selling back the Porsche felt almost as good as buying it in the first place. Why? Because the things you own weigh you down. They need to be maintained and looked after. Before long they might become outdated and need to be replaced. And the more we spend on them, the more we worry about them. Again, ask yourself: who is the owner in this scenario? Are you running your life or is it running you?

Of course, we all need a comfortable place to live, a means of transport, and clothes that fit the environment we work in, or which make us feel good about ourselves. But if we are honest, a lot of the things we pursue are because we want them rather than because we need them. Because we were influenced by a clever advertisement. Because someone else we knew got one. Because we thought it would make us happier, healthier, or more attractive.

It's another of those ideas that gets implanted from a young age. Save your pocket money for long enough and you can afford the game, shoes, or gadget all your friends have been telling you about. As we grow up, we do the same with our salaries. The psychology doesn't change, just the size of the prize and how much it costs.

Like hard work that isn't attached to a purpose and a dream, this is a dead end. Eventually you get the long-awaited possession and maybe it does make you happy for a while. But soon you're bored with your new toy, it's proving more trouble than you expected, and a part of you wonders why you fell for the hype in the first place.

It's the fast-food approach to life. The idea of the meal is usually so much better than the reality. That's the truth about possessions. You want them, sometimes you will get them, but for the most part you don't need them. And you'll be happy without them. Even if you think a house, a car, or a swimming pool in the garden is your dream, I promise you it isn't. Chasing possessions will only get in the way of finding your real dream in life.

Those, then, are the myths we are told about life and why we need to escape them. To start moving towards your dream, first you need to free yourself from the belief that hard work will solve all your problems, that failure is to be feared, that difficult things are to be avoided, and that possessions are what you seek. You have to weed out these ideas to make space for the dream to take root.

But what of the dream? And what *is* a dream, a real one? Why does it matter? Why is this the question that I am imploring you to ask yourself? Normally we start something at the beginning. But the whole point of the dream, the whole purpose of this exercise, is for you to start at the end. So, shall we?

2

Why a Dream Matters

Of all the entrepreneurs I have known, from those I've met across a boardroom table to others I've discovered while walking down main streets with my microphone, few have inspired me more than Kellie. She was one of the early people who pitched her dream to the doorbell and her story blew me away.

It was a simple idea. Kellie was a dog groomer and she wanted to launch her own business rather than working for someone else. She cared passionately about the animals she worked with and wanted an environment that would allow her to look after the dogs the way she knew best. She already had a brilliant name for this business: Kellie's K9s.

So far, so good. But there was something else about Kellie, something that told me she was more than a frustrated employee who wanted to become her own boss. When she agreed to meet me and talk about her dream, it soon became clear what this was. Still in her early twenties, Kellie had already overcome more challenges than many people three times her age. Her dad had died when she was a young child and her mother then remarried to a stepfather whom Kellie found challenging. When a court ordered him to leave the country, her mum went with him. As a teenager, she had effectively been abandoned and become homeless. When we spoke, in an interview she agreed to publish, she told me about the day a social worker had come to her school to tell her that her mother was leaving.

"I had to learn independence from a young age," she told me. "If I didn't look out for me, no one else was [going to]." The experience had left Kellie not only with the skills of self-reliance, but a desire to provide care—"being able to help something that can't speak up when it needs help," as she described her work with animals.

Her story had made clear how deeply rooted this dream was in her life experiences. She didn't just talk about working with animals, but also nurturing them, caring for them, and looking after them in a way no one else would—in the way she must have wished someone had looked after her. "There's a massive welfare side to it," she said. "Groomers will notice things about animals that pet owners might not notice. Lumps, bumps, skin problems." For her, this business was about doing the one thing she truly loved and, through it, trying to help those without the power to help themselves.

The way Kellie had taken the greatest pain of her life and made something out of it, turning that pain into purpose, was both instructive and inspirational. It showed the immense power of a dream that grows out of personal experience—a wrong we wish to right in the world or a difference we want to make. Because Kellie was so clear about her plan and it was rooted in purpose, I didn't doubt for a moment that she would succeed. Even when she experienced a setback, struggling to find an appropriate space for her dog salon, I knew she would find a way. Soon she had—a van that allowed her to launch a mobile salon and take her business on the road, making it even more convenient for her customers. Kellie's K9s had been born. Her beautiful dream had taken flight.

Kellie's story is a great example of the power of a dream—how it can focus and inspire you, lifting your sights and helping you clear obstacles out of your path. It shows how we can combine our worst experiences and biggest hopes into something that will give shape and direction to our life. And it helps to explain why I spend so much time going around asking people a very specific question.

Not "what's your goal in life?"

Not "what do you want to achieve?"

Not "what's your biggest ambition?"

Instead, each and every time, I choose the same word: do you have a *dream*? What's your *dream*?

I have asked this question of thousands of people—online and walking the streets with a microphone. I've asked it from Trafalgar Square to Times Square, at festivals and in fast-food shops, to people who were crossing the street and others who were crossing the ocean at 35,000 feet. Asking that question and listening to people's answers has changed the way I think about life, success, and happiness. It's opened my eyes to the amazing potential that every one of us has, and also to the barriers that so many of us place in the way of achieving it.

I ask it like this because I believe the word "dream" is one of the most powerful in our language.

Consider some examples. The idea that powered some of the most incredible businesses, the most dramatic scientific discoveries, and the most brilliant creativity of the last century wasn't the American Goal or the American Promise. It was the American Dream.

Civil rights leader Dr. Martin Luther King didn't inspire millions of people by declaring that he had a plan. He said, "I have a *dream*."

The idea of the dream is influential. It is provocative. It makes us stop and think, lingering in our mind long after it has been spoken.

Part of the reason is that the dream has an element of the taboo. Lots of people are afraid to say that they have one. It risks marking you out as someone unserious, arrogant, and presumptuous. Who are you to have a dream? What makes you think you are entitled to that?

This attitude stems directly from the myths we have just talked about. The compulsion to keep your head down, work hard, and wait for the world to reward you rather than going out and getting it. It makes people afraid to admit their dream, even to themselves. For many, there is also a feeling that there is just not enough time to be aspirational: there are jobs to do and bills to pay.

That's why I ask the question the way I do. It's a key to unlock that prison and give us the permission to say out loud the thing we have often thought about, but maybe have never shared. With my microphone, I go and talk to people working in supermarkets, doing security on doors, or just crossing the road. I catch them in the middle of their day, following a routine. Not everyone knows how to react or wants to answer the question.

But with lots of people, something miraculous happens. Their eyes come alive. They stand a little taller and tell me about the brand they want to launch and the culture they want it to celebrate, about their plans to travel the world, to launch a photography business, a coffee shop with a purpose, a drop-in service for people in crisis. Often, I think I am talking to a different person than the one I approached only seconds before. The transformation is immediate and straight away it tells us something about the power of a dream. How

it can change the way we think about the world and ourselves.

Take Delon, who was working at McDonald's when I met
him. As he handed me my food, I asked him my question.

"A dream? Not really, no."

The look on his face told me that no one had ever asked him
anything like this before. I wasn't convinced by his answer and
decided to push a little further. What about the future, what
did he want to achieve?

He shrugged: there was no plan, no dream, he was just living his life and seeing where it would lead.

I still didn't really believe him. I thought there was probably
more to Delon's story, but he wasn't ready to share it yet. So I
changed tack and switched my question to an offer. I was going
to sit down and eat my food. If he could think of his dream and
come and tell me about it before I left, I would help him make
it happen.

It turned out that he was coming to the end of his shift, and
within ten minutes he had appeared at my table, big coat on,
bag of chips and can of Coke in hand. More than his outfit had
changed. Delon had too. He was smiling, confident, and didn't
hesitate.

"I think I've come up with my dream. My dream is to be a
Twitch streamer. A popular one, make people smile."

Just as I had doubted him saying that he didn't have a dream, I
believed Delon now. When he sat down and we spoke some
more, I learned that he had been afraid to share this idea with his
friends or family. He thought they wouldn't take him seriously
and that he would be laughed at for saying he wanted to make his
living as a gamer. In fact, I was the first person he'd ever told.
Soon he discovered that those fears had been misplaced. People
were listening in to our conversation and encouraging him. His

manager even said he wanted to help him. When I uploaded a video about Delon, the number of people hearing his story and supporting him reached millions.

It was remarkable watching a person come to life like this, giving voice to their dream, and seeing that people wanted to cheer him on and help him. That is the power of a dream: the expression of our deepest (and sometimes most secret) desire in life, the ambition we have always nurtured even if we have rarely spoken about it. It's an image of the best version of our lives, something that can change how others see us and how we think about ourselves.

Most of us have some concept of this. But too many of us then do something bizarre. **We put our dream away and forget about it.** We treat it as a guilty pleasure to be hidden rather than a burning ambition to be chased after. We talk down our chances and give up without trying.

That's not necessarily our fault. There are plenty of voices and influences telling us that a dream is fanciful and we should accept our lot. The constant message is to put your head down, pass your exams, get qualified, and keep working hard towards the next promotion. That's advice given with good intentions, but it discourages you from the things that you need to achieve a dream—like standing out from the crowd, pursuing your own ideas, taking risks, and embracing failure.

Because we all go through this training, being told that our value is determined by our school and career achievements and not our passions in life, we often become distrustful of our dreams, if we have even admitted to them. We tell ourselves that we're not good enough to achieve them. That it's better not to try than to risk failure and lose face. Even if we don't completely discount the possibility of success, we may put it off for another day or another year—in some cases another life.

The paradox of our dreams is that **the thing we most want in life is often the thing we are most afraid of doing**. So often, we take one of the most miraculous human abilities— the capacity to imagine what the future could be—and we use it against ourselves. We imagine this beautiful future and then we deny ourselves the chance to pursue it. We say that our deepest desire isn't possible, and that it's better to forget about it.

This is one of our most self-defeating traits as humans, because there is no better way to think about your life or approach the future than to frame it in terms of a dream.

This is so much more than an idea. It is a power source, like plugging yourself into the mains when you have been running for all this time on half-empty batteries. When you have a dream in your life, you never need to question why you are doing something or if it is worthwhile. You already know—it is taking you one step closer to the thing you want to achieve and the person you want to be.

A dream may be a simple thing, something that can and should be expressed in a sentence. But it is also multifaceted, supporting us in all sorts of ways as we go through life. Let's look at some of those now—the reasons why I believe this is the most important question that you can ask yourself, and what you gain when you are brave enough to come up with an answer.

Why dream? An end and a start

A few pages ago I told you that having a dream means starting at the end. Well, it's a little more complicated than that.

Here's the truthful part of that statement. Part of a dream's power is that it takes us to a different place from the one we are currently in. Whatever the struggles of our life—trying to find work, to pay bills, to achieve qualifications, to have a family—the big idea lifts us beyond them. Not for good, but for long enough that we can glimpse what a better future may look like. It allows us to see the finish line in the race we are about to run. It provides motivation.

Your dream can do this and it also has the power to inspire others. One of the most exciting things about my work is how, when I help one individual, I can also share their story with millions of others. My DMs are flooded with messages from people who have started their own business or side hustle after being inspired by someone in one of my videos.

One time I posted a video where a sixteen-year-old approached me on the street to share his business idea—motorized toy cars for kids. Six months later, I received this DM from another young person: "My dad told me I should get a job at Tesco's [that's the grocery store where he works] and not waste time on my expensive hobby. Since I watched your video of the boy dreaming of selling motorized cars, and saw that your hobby could be your business, I realized there is a good business in my hobby car business. I now make more money in one month than my dad did all year and love it so much."

That was one person's dream in action, giving confidence and belief to someone who hadn't yet dared to embrace theirs. That is the power of our imagination, which a dream allows us to harness. If you can't imagine a better future, then you are never going to achieve it. Yet this vital "muscle" in our brain, one we all developed and exercised as children, is one that too many of us allow to waste away with age. You need a dream to build it up again.

Now for the clever bit. Even though we're thinking about

the future, something we haven't attained and which may take years to realize, **we can start right now**. The dream is right there and there is nothing stopping us from taking the first step towards it. That is the genius of our human ability to predict and imagine the future—to think about what it may be like. It's both distant and accessible. An end and a start. Knowing where you want to finish is also an invitation to make a beginning.

A dream's capacity to change our perception of reality, even briefly, is one of its most important features. Because it is open to anyone. You don't need money, a job, qualifications, or even a roof over your head. Dreams are democratic and they are universal. Indeed they are even more important to people who have little, or nothing, than to those who are already living a comfortable life.

The name Chris Gardner may or may not be familiar to you, but you probably remember the film made about his life, *The Pursuit of Happyness*. In the book it was based on, he wrote about finding his dream at the lowest point of his life. As a 27-year-old single dad, he had a job but no place to live, unable to afford either rent or childcare. For a year, he and his son, Chris Jr., were homeless—sleeping under the desk in his office, in airport waiting areas, church shelters, and even a train station bathroom. With one hand he pushed his child's buggy, and with the other he carried a duffel bag with all their possessions and a suit carrier with his spare work clothes.

Then his dream, quite literally, pulled up to the sidewalk in a glittering red Ferrari. He stopped the man who got out and asked him what he had done to get this amazing-looking car. He was a stockbroker. So Gardner decided to become one too. He saw his way out of despair, and later started a brokerage firm that he sold for millions of dollars, before becoming a globally renowned motivational speaker. It was having a dream, he wrote, that had sustained him and helped him and his son to survive their perilous situation. "As long as I kept my mental focus on destinations that were ahead, destinations that I had the audacity to dream might hold a red Ferrari of my own, I protected myself from despair . . . as long as I kept moving forward, one foot in front of the other, the voices of fear and shame, the messages from those who wanted me to believe that I wasn't good enough, would be stilled."[1]

It's an incredible example of what a dream can help a person to achieve (and that there's no harm in including a possession in there as long as it's linked to a purpose, and that you don't rely on the possession part to make you happy).

To imagine and to dream are universal human abilities—not one passed down between generations or accredited by a university. We can all do it. The only question is whether we permit ourselves to do it and are willing to follow where it takes us.

Wherever you are in life, a dream gives you a place to start because it provides you with a target to aim for. It harnesses that great human skill of predicting the future, not against us but for us. It allows us to imagine, permits us to hope, and enables us to believe. What better starting point could there possibly be than that?

Why dream? It keeps you going

A dream may give you a destination to aim for, but quickly you find yourself wondering how you are going to get there. You realize that, however confident you are, it is going to be hard.

That is why you need to start with a dream rather than a plan, a goal, an objective, or a hope. Because getting things done in life is difficult, you need the right kind of motivation to succeed. One that doesn't just tide you over for a few days or weeks, but which will keep you going for years and years, through doubt and adversity.

Whatever we choose to commit ourselves to, we are going to face problems along the way. If you run a business, you will lose customers, employees will leave, other people will get selected ahead of you, competitors will emerge, and mistakes will be made. Some of your ideas will fail, and you will kick yourself about opportunities you missed. You might wake up one morning to find that the world has suddenly changed around you because of war, disease, or extreme weather. Any or all of these things will happen to you at some point in your life.

It's at moments like these that the dream comes into its own. It provides a real anchor for the long term, not just for this week, the next quarter, or the coming year. It is bigger than the problems you currently face and cannot be destroyed by the adversity that has arrived on your doorstep (unless you let it).

That much was amply demonstrated by one of the most remarkable people of our times, the education campaigner Malala Yousafzai, youngest ever winner of the Nobel Peace Prize. When she was eleven, the Taliban took over her town in northern Afghanistan and decreed among other things that women and girls would not be allowed an education. They shut down the school. But Malala kept going, and started to speak out about why this was so wrong. She became sufficiently well known that the extremists tried to stop her. In 2012, she was targeted and shot on her school bus, narrowly escaping death.

"So, yes, the Taliban have shot me. But they can only shoot a body," she later wrote of the experience and how it drove her on to redouble her efforts as an activist. "They cannot shoot my dreams, they cannot kill my beliefs, and they cannot stop my campaign to see every girl and every boy in school."[2]

Almost none of us will have to endure anything nearly as extreme, traumatic, and life-changing as Malala did. But we can all learn from her example, and her belief in the power of the dream, something that only got stronger when people who hated that dream tried to stop her through the most violent means possible.

That is what a dream is capable of—it enables you not just to survive adversity but to grow through it. If you can hold on to your dream as you experience all of life's setbacks, then it and you become stronger as a result. Because the dream is still intact, you are still here, and if those things aren't going to stop you then perhaps nothing will.

This is where a dream differs from and stands above its more familiar cousins: the targets we set ourselves, the resolutions we make, and the goals we hope to achieve. I can almost guarantee that everyone reading this has had versions of these in their lives. And almost everyone will know what it is like for them to fail. Targets are missed, goals are shelved or altered, and resolutions are surrendered when we can feel our willpower beginning to drain away.

That is the problem with these concepts, the most popular models for thinking about and approaching the future. They are short- or medium-term at best: once we are done (or not done) with this year's goals and targets, we will adopt new ones, often without pausing to think about what we learned last time. They are binary, like exams that we are either going to pass or fail. And because they have a 50/50 chance of failure, they are brittle—almost as if they were designed for us to give up on them.

In comparison, a dream is engineered for the long term and

built for survival. It's often your destiny. It's meant to be and you will fight to achieve it unless the system stops you. You can have a bad month, even a bad year, without giving up. You can switch paths and change careers and still be working to achieve it. No one is going to sit you down for an annual dream review and tell you that, unfortunately, your performance has not been up to scratch.

Your dream lives and moves with you. It is big enough to contain failure, to allow for diversions, and to enable multiple course corrections. It doesn't just inspire you to get started and to keep going, giving you something to keep moving towards. It also declines to punish you when things go wrong, or if you fail and have to start again. You might have moments of real and painful failure, but your dream doesn't die with them. It persists, and if you persist with it, you will find new outlets for it and the determination to try again.

A dream can be your companion, spurring you on to the next thing and picking you up when you fall. By drawing us on to the future and lifting our sights beyond the circumstances we are currently in, it gives us something we need but can't always find—a dose of perspective, telling us that we are not as good as we think, nor are the problems we currently face as big as they seem. A dream should curtail your overconfidence at the same time as quelling your fears. Because it never goes away, you can rely on it to ensure you keep moving forward, however long and rambling the route.

Why dream? It makes you believe

"I had $106 in the bank. Things were not looking very good. My $40 car had just blown up and I was taking a bus to work."[3]

Those are not the words you expect from someone who has just turned down an offer of over $300,000 to buy a script they have written. But this was no ordinary script, and no ordinary person. It was *Rocky*, and the author was Sylvester Stallone. He wanted the money, of course, and he wanted his movie to be made. The problem? He also wanted to star in it.

Today, it feels unthinkable that anyone else but Stallone could have played the underdog fighter who would be the basis of a billion-dollar movie franchise. Back in the mid-1970s, it was also unthinkable to Stallone. He had been inspired to write the script after watching the 1975 bout between Muhammad Ali and Chuck Wepner, a heavyweight known more for taking punches than landing them, so much so that he was nicknamed the "Bayonne Bleeder." But Wepner had not gone down easily against "The Greatest." He had lasted almost the entire fifteen rounds, and famously put Ali on the canvas in the ninth.

Stallone completed the script in just three days. But he didn't just want to write. He wanted to act. And he wanted to act *this part*—the one he had been compelled to write because he felt it reflected him and his frustrations in life: someone down on their luck, thought of as muscle and nothing more, begging for an opportunity that seemed like it might never arrive. Getting the script sold wasn't his purpose. Having that story told— the way he wanted—was. Somehow he knew it was his best chance, perhaps his only chance, to fulfill his dream of becoming a Hollywood actor. "There was something inside of me [that said] you know, this opportunity is never going to come around [again]," he later reflected.

The producers had other ideas. They wanted someone who was already a star, not a guy who thought he could be one. Their casting list for Rocky was full of big names—Robert Redford, Burt Reynolds, James Caan—and Stallone had no name. His acting career was going nowhere. In fact, he'd first got these producers interested in the script after a failed audition, when he mentioned on the way out that he had also been doing some writing.

It should have been an easy problem to solve. Stallone had no money (he'd even had to sell his dog because he couldn't afford to buy its food) and the producers had plenty. They wouldn't need to throw much in his direction to get him to budge. Would they? The first offer, Stallone remembered, was for $25,000. When he said no, it kept going up: $75,000, $100,000, $250,000. Still, he stood his ground and refused. It was his story and he had to be the one to tell it. That was his dream. Without the part, there wouldn't be a deal.

It sounds like something you can't believe, that a person with not enough money to pay next month's rent would turn down a sum that would allow him to buy several houses. But Stallone's rationale was clear. "I know in the back of my mind, if I sell this script and it does very, very well [and I'm not in it], I'm going to jump off a building." He plucked up his courage, and kept saying no.

"No" is such a powerful word. I wish more people said no to bad advice or crappy job offers. Stallone embraced this power. He told himself that even though it felt illogical, it would work out, later saying: "[This] is one of those things where you just roll the dice and fly by the proverbial seat of your pants and I may be totally wrong, and I'm going to be taking a lot of people down with me [if I am], but I just believe in it."

I just believe in it.

Five words that sum up the power of a dream and the gift it gives you: a rock-solid core of belief. When you are doing something for a reason, and when you truly believe in that purpose, then there is almost nothing you will allow to stop you.

You will keep trying, keep negotiating, keep experimenting and enduring failure to get what you want and fulfill your objective. Because you believe in what you are doing.

Stallone was willing to turn down offer after life-changing offer because he knew what he really wanted. Not a payday to alleviate his financial woes, but the opportunity he had been waiting years for, the chance to tell his story, which he knew so many others shared. He knew that to have taken the money and handed over the part would have been surrendering his purpose and selling his dream. Missing the one opportunity that some instinct said was going to be the making of him.

We all know his belief paid off. He got the part, and the money, and went on to become one of the biggest Hollywood names of his era. He did it because he had that most precious asset a dream can give to a person: belief in himself and belief in his ideas.

It's that kind of belief we all need when we set out to achieve something. There are always difficulties, there is always competition, and there is never a shortage of reasons to give up. Through all of that, you will not survive and **you will not achieve what you want if you don't truly believe in it**. A belief that says it doesn't matter what people or life throw at you, or how many rejections you pile up along the way. You will carry on, because your dream is clear and your faith in it is undiminished.

Sometimes no one is going to believe in an idea but you. Sometimes no one is going to believe in *you* except you. That's the point at which the person without a dream quits, and the one who has it steels themselves to carry on. Because while you still have belief, you will never give up.

That is the beauty of having a dream in your life. It not only makes you more ambitious about the future but equips you to be more resilient, confident, and steadfast as you move towards it. With a dream, you swap the treadmill of a salary and a mortgage for something bigger and far more rewarding. A personal cause you will dedicate your life to achieving. Something that will make work seem like fun, and help difficult tasks become achievable. The closest thing we have in life to real alchemy.

I go around the world asking people about their dreams because I never stop being amazed at how these ideas can transform body language and bring some inner spirit alive. I believe that we all want to dream and we are all meant to, but too many of us think we shouldn't or are waiting for someone to give them permission. Well, I'm giving it to you. And through this book I'm going to help you work out your dream and how to achieve it.

Step one on that journey was understanding society's myths and why we need to move past them. And step two is tapping into the thing that drives the dream: the gasoline in its engine, powering you through every day and each new challenge. That fuel is purpose, and finding it is our next priority.

3.

Why Purpose Matters

When my team and I go out filming, we never know who we're going to meet. Even as I watch people rushing past on the street or in a shopping center, I'm not sure who I'm going to try to speak to next. I don't always know what draws me to step into that person's path and ask them about their dream. I also have no idea how they are going to respond.

That's half the fun of the job: each story comes as a surprise, and often there is a great wisdom behind it, from people who haven't rehearsed what they are about to say and truly speak from the heart.

A great example came while filming one afternoon in a train station. A man was walking past: tall, well-built, dressed in black, with sleeve tattoos, moustache, and a shaved head. Not necessarily the kind of person you'd think about interrupting for a chat. But some instinct told me that I should. Soon he was telling me his story. His name was Bradley and he'd been a helicopter engineer in the British Army. Now he worked as a sports massage therapist. Looking closer, I could see the name of his business printed on his T-shirt: The Massage Guys.

This hadn't just been a career change, but an awakening of something deeper. "I want to help people get out of pain," he told me. "That's the main sort of goal for my life really." As an engineer, Bradley had been stuck in a rut: you fixed one machine and were thanked by being given the next one to work on. Fixing people was different, he said. You get gratitude, you feel good because you know you have taken someone's pain away, and you can't wait to help the next person. The work becomes its own reward.

The way Bradley told his story, with clarity and humility, told me that he had found something we all need—a counterpart to our dream and something that will be required to achieve it. This is purpose, our essential reason for being, the motive that keeps us ticking over and moving forward as we work towards the dream. His purpose was fixing people and taking away their pain.

Bradley didn't just tell me about his own purpose. He also shared a perfect summary of how and why we should search for this very precious asset. "Give more and try different ways of giving. And when you find that one thing that gives you a warm feeling, run with that." That is a beautiful sentiment, which chimes with one of my all-time favorite quotes: "The purpose of life is a life of purpose."

It is purpose I want to talk about now, because this is something you will need to fulfill your dream. It's a close cousin to it, but not the same thing, and it will be important to your journey in different ways.

To explain what purpose is and why we need it, let me go back to the story of Fluid, the creative agency Helen and I built in Hong Kong. It was the most successful business of my career—the one that I worked longest in and made the most money from. There were lots of reasons for that success, including that we filled a market gap for digital design at a time when the internet was beginning to take off for businesses. But we weren't the only company doing this, and when we started there was at least one established competitor working out of a lavish office, while we had barely two desks to call our own.

To begin with, I thought that filling our niche would be enough: that we could outwork the competition and that the success of a business was down to nothing more than supplying the right service at the right price (and of course putting in all that hard work we've talked about). But I was wrong and Fluid almost failed because of it.

In the early years, we appeared to be doing well. We signed major clients like CNN and Estée Lauder and work was steady. The business grew. But one problem wouldn't go away: our people kept leaving. We were regularly short-staffed, losing clients and turning down work as a result.

For a long time, I was in denial about this. I said that people didn't get it, that they hadn't been the right hires in the first place, and that we would find others who could do the job better. This can happen to entrepreneurs: the business is their life and they struggle to understand that other people might care less about it than they do.

Eventually, the pattern became so clear that I could not deny it any longer. I started talking to the people who had decided to leave. Soon, I realized I should have been doing this from the beginning. The feedback was clear and consistent. In their minds, our business had no purpose. We were just helping other people to make money. It wasn't fulfilling and there was no greater reason to stay late or go the extra mile for clients.

Initially, I pushed back. There was a purpose, I said—we worked with brilliant companies and helped them to succeed and tell their stories to the world. This was a weak argument and soon I had stopped believing it myself. Finally, I listened, and together Helen and I did a lot of soul searching about the business and what we wanted it to stand for.

It took us back to the reason we had started Fluid in the first place. It was Helen. She was a talented creative but was regularly taken advantage of by customers who lowballed her on price. She was doing brilliant work and not charging enough for it. She wasn't alone in this: creative people often get a raw deal because negotiating fees and compensation isn't necessarily part of their skill set. That was the basis for our business: let designers do what they do best, and let someone else worry about looking after them.

That had been our purpose at the beginning but along the way it had become lost. No longer. We made a decision: instead of being a company focused on helping brands make even more money, we would be one that celebrated creativity. We wanted to put the people who did the important things for these brands on a pedestal and give them the environment they needed to do their best work. Not through pats on the back and neck massages, but by making sure people were paid what they were worth, and telling clients that they couldn't have the job done in a rush if they wanted it done well. We tried to take away the two overwhelming pressures of any creative's working life: not getting paid properly and not having enough time to do the work. After that, we never had a major staff turnover problem again.

This purpose ran through everything. It informed the people we hired, the clients we went after, and our culture as a business. Over time it developed our reputation with the two audiences that mattered most: creatives heard that we were a good place to work, and clients knew us as an agency that did everything thoroughly. It meant we avoided the biggest trap of our industry, where you are so eager to please the customer that you end up making life miserable for your own people, who then leave and tell their peers not to work with you.

Think about the difference between working hard and working with purpose. The hard work you notice: all those long hours, fruitless pitches, and extra miles for demanding clients. How could you not? But purpose, the secret ingredient, works silently. When you have it, it's almost effortless and leaves no trace—like flour in a cake, you can't taste it at the end, but good luck trying to get anywhere without it.

Purpose was that ingredient at Fluid. People wanted to work with us because we had it. We weren't just creating a logo, designing a brochure, or building a website; we were doing something we all believed in, which was to create a better environment for the kind of work we loved doing. We were building something. It's why one of the most popular quotes in business is the idea that "culture eats strategy for breakfast." Your culture, which grows out of your purpose and how people apply it in their everyday work, is the thing that attracts people to a company and then keeps them there.

That is the quiet magic of purpose in the business context. It's the rope that everyone can hold on to as you climb the mountain. It connects a team of people and organizes them towards a common goal. It is galvanizing, motivating, and unifying.

This is an asset we all need. And it derives directly from your dream. A dream doesn't stand on its own. It's not a disconnected cloud floating through the sky, but something deeply rooted in your life experience, your wants and needs. Nor will it be achieved without the right focus and motivation—one that lives with you every day, propelling you towards an aim that can often seem distant. That is what purpose provides.

You can have many purposes and all of them provide fuel for the dream, which is singular. To use myself as an example, my dream is to help create a world in which the #GiveWithoutTake mindset of people helping people becomes widespread. That one dream contains multiple purposes, including to fix the education system, to help other people find their dream, and to ignite ten million of those dreams.

My dream is big—a point on the horizon—and my purposes provide pathways to get me there. The dream gets you started and gives you that destination to aim for, but purpose is what keeps you going, day after day, year after year. If the dream is like the brain, a source of imagination and feeling, then purpose is the heart, pumping blood and maintaining the beat. They are closely linked but perform separate functions. And you need the two together, working closely in tandem.

That purpose starts with you; then, as you build a team and a business, it can connect lots of other people to that dream. (But only if the purpose is authentic. There is a lot of fake purpose in the world, and people can see it a mile off.)

In this chapter, we'll look at purpose in more detail: what it is, how it works, and why you must have it to achieve your dream.

Why purpose? It charges your battery

When we use the word "purpose" it can sound a bit pretentious. Like it's something for people with too much time on their hands. An optional extra that's nice if you can get it.

That perception couldn't be more wrong. Purpose is essential to our well-being, something that can make a difference not just to our happiness but to our health. We flourish with purpose and suffer in its absence.

The search for purpose begins with a closely related issue:

our motivations. We all have these. Whatever anyone tells you, there aren't motivated and unmotivated people in life. But there are healthy and unhealthy motivations.

The classic unhealthy one is what I call "burnout motivation." You say that your purpose in life is to feed your family. Pay your mortgage. Keep your head above water. You make these necessities your focus and call it purpose. The problem with that approach is that you are setting yourself up on a treadmill that you can't turn off. At best, you have managed to survive and tick over for another month. At worst, you have failed and let people down. It's a recipe for waking up every day feeling tired. Forcing yourself out of the door and through the working day.

This situation is the worst of all worlds—where you are working hard without a purpose that fulfills and nourishes you. You put everything in and you get nothing back except keeping the wolf from the door.

Having a purpose puts you in the opposite position. The long evenings of dread and the snooze button on your alarm are banished. You actually look forward to going to work. You stop talking about "work-life balance." Why? Because you are doing something you want to do. Something that feels worth doing: a proper use of your time, effort, and skill. And all this effort doesn't feel like it's going down the drain, or straight into someone else's pocket. It's helping you, moving you closer to your dream. The work you do becomes an investment: a down payment on the future you are trying to create rather than a routine that sucks up your energy and will to live.

This is the key point about purpose: the way it changes the relationship between what we do and how we feel. Think of your willpower, your morale, and your mental health as like a battery. Everything you do will either charge it up or run it down. Burnout motivation means that you are draining your battery every day of every week.

By contrast, pure purpose—the good kind of motivation—restores that battery even when you are working like a dog. Studies of groups from firefighters in Poland to Catholic priests in Italy have found that those with an expressed sense of purpose were less likely to experience burnout and struggle with the challenges of their work.[1] Having a purpose doesn't just help you to feel better about your life and what you are doing, it also allows you to do more. Like a runner with carbon plates in their shoes versus one with weights tied onto them.

Having purpose makes your life better. It may even save your life. A study that tracked the health of more than 13,000 Americans over the age of fifty found that those with the strongest sense of purpose also had the lowest risk of mortality.[2] Another one showed that people with more purpose were less likely to have to spend time in the hospital.[3] So believe me when I tell you that purpose not only has the capacity to change your life, it might just have the power to keep you alive.

Why purpose? It solves the other problems

Perhaps as you read this, you already know what your purpose in life is. Perhaps you have an inkling but have not yet fully explored the ideas.

Or perhaps you believe that you have no purpose and will struggle to find one.

When I meet people in this third group, they often give one of the following explanations:

I haven't got time to dream.

I don't care.

I'm too lazy.

I need money before I can have a dream.

None of these things are really true, or at least none of them can't be changed. The things people say about not having a purpose, or not being able to have one, are generally a list of excuses, self-made prisons, and misconceptions. More about those in the next chapter.

I often see people looking at their peers who are doing well and thinking: *that's not me. I'm not built that way. It's OK for them.*

Unfortunately, and this is one of the times I need to be blunt, this is yet again another lie. It's one of those stories we tell to make ourselves feel better. To surrender agency over our lives and say it was all decided by someone or something else—by circumstances, by genetics, by luck.

In addition to asking people what their dream is on the street, I have interviewed over 200 of the world's most successful people on my podcast. These conversations showed me that the difference between people who succeed and those who believe themselves to be failing isn't something magical or God-given. It isn't innate or immutable. It's simple and by now you know what it is: it's having an unshakeable mission. A purpose.

That's the difference. Because inside each one of us is a lazy person, a self-doubting person, a jealous and an insecure person. Lacking a purpose makes it all too easy to give in to these negative voices. To revert to our factory settings and become self-pitying or self-blaming. It exposes us to distractions, to bad habits, and to a cycle in which we can never escape the limitations we place on ourselves.

The purposeful person isn't fundamentally different—except in one way. They have a focus in their life, a thing they want to do, a goal they wish to achieve, and a dream they want to pursue.

Having that good motivation (wherever it comes from) tops up your energy and makes you eager to run towards the next opportunity. People with this are difficult to distract, to knock off course, or to get down for long. They have taken the closest thing there is to a magic pill in life, simply by equipping themselves with the power of purpose.

That is the inconvenient truth. The reasons you think you can't have a purpose are all problems solved by having, you guessed it, purpose.

That is the second great asset of a purpose in life. As well as giving you energy where so many things in life sap it, purpose provides you with focus. It tightens your perspective and sharpens your mindset.

There's a reason that the person you secretly envy in your peer group or workplace seems to be able to do it all. The business or side hustle, the early-morning gym sessions, the voluntary work, and the family time. It's because they are already purposeful and can transfer that quality into every corner of their life.

I encountered a beautiful example of this while visiting New York. We were filming and to be honest it felt like an unpromising day. The Manhattan sky was gray. In fact, everything looked gray, from the sidewalk below us to the skyscrapers towering in the background. Then I spotted a blast of color striding out of this drab background. A middle-aged woman was approaching, her hair dyed red and her dress a striking teal blue. I had to talk to her, and was soon glad that I had.

Her dream was to raise money, and she was going to achieve it through her work as an artist. Why did she want the money? Not for possessions or status, but for a much deeper purpose. A two-time cancer survivor, she wanted to make money so she could help to fund cancer research and treatment. "I always say, if ever I become a millionaire, my first priority before anything else is to donate to cancer research," she told me.

I met this lady for no more than two minutes. But, as she showed me a photo of one of her paintings, on display in New York's Bellevue Hospital, I realized what a powerful purpose she had harnessed in her life. A purpose that had come through pain. "I felt it happened for a reason, because if [cancer] hadn't happened to me, I wouldn't have discovered this," she said, meaning her art. Her dream was to help eradicate cancer, and her purpose—the thing that was going to help her achieve that—was her painting. That purpose to make art and use it to help others suffering as she had was now the fundamental motivation of her life.

When you have a purpose like this, you are less inclined to waste time because you know you have important things to do. You are less likely to give in to temptation because it may distract you from your goal. You are less likely to doubt yourself to the point of inaction, because you already know what you wish to achieve, and are not daunted by the possibility of failing on the way.

That's why purpose is the great problem solver. All those issues that some of us wallow in are negated by purpose. Bad habits, distractions, and doubts lose their power over us. Finding your purpose is one of the best favors you will ever do for yourself. Doing it clears away so much of the harmful clutter that surrounds our lives and fills our heads, and creates the space to focus on what actually matters. It paves the way towards the dream.

Why purpose? It makes each day worthwhile

Whether we like it or not, most of us will spend most of our time working. Your dream is only going to be achieved through work of some kind. The question is: can you find purpose in your work? Can you make it fun—something you actually want to do, and that carries more positive associations than negative?

When the US-based Bureau of Labor Statistics gathers data about work, it asks people to rank what they do on several scales, including happiness, meaning, and stress. Across several surveys from 2010 to 2021, the three most meaningful industries were, in order: agriculture, logging, and forestry; health and social assistance; and educational services.[4]

In other words, the people who found their work to be most purposeful were those helping to feed people, to look after people when they are ill, and to teach young people. These are not the easiest jobs or the best paid. Those working in health and education were far from the top of the table when it came to happiness. But their jobs are meaningful. They contain purpose. They allow people to do what feels like a good day's work, and then to go back and do it again even when conditions are hard and the circumstances far from perfect.

I hear the same thing all the time from people working as nurses, firefighters, or police officers. Their jobs are hard, but they mostly love doing them because they find purpose in helping people and making a difference every day of their lives. Of the thousands of people I have interviewed, these are the people who most often seem happy with their lives. In fact, I make a point of asking police officers about their dream when I see them, and I am yet to meet one who does not say that they are already living it. I've never met a banker or a lawyer who feels the same way.

That is an important example of the role purpose plays in an everyday sense. Not in the highlights reel we post on Instagram, the image we curate of our life, but in the reality of having to turn up day after day, keeping going even when it's cold, you're tired, and you know that something difficult is sitting on your desk.

Our lives can't be inspirational all the time. You're not going to feel fulfilled with every email you send or even every sale you make. None of us can escape the fact that there are bills to be paid, calls to be made, lunchboxes to be packed, and clothes to be washed.

And that is exactly why we need purpose—the knowledge that we are pursuing something worthwhile, even if the thing we are doing right now feels mundane. It means a completely fruitless day, or one spent doing the most boring part of your job, can still be a good day's work. Because you were fulfilling your purpose, and through it moving a step closer to achieving your dream.

One morning at Fluid we were preparing to welcome an important group of people to our office. This was a client we had been trying to land for years and at last we had secured the meeting that might lead to a dream project. Then our cleaner called in sick. I went into the bathroom in the office and realized we couldn't leave it like it was with important guests coming to visit us. So I put rubber gloves on and cleaned the toilets myself. And it was the best thing I did that week to help the business. I had an hour's work cleaning toilets because, even though it wasn't what I wanted to be doing, it helped us get closer to the thing we really did want. That's a good metaphor for life. Sometimes we have to clean up shit to win. You won't mind doing it if your purpose is clear.

That is another way in which purpose is so important. It's a form of armor that means the boring, bad, and baffling bits of life affect us less. We can embrace the tedious, tackle the difficult, and overcome the unpleasant if we remind ourselves that it is all contributing to something bigger than the problem you face that day. Like most things in life, you can do them better if you know what you are doing them for.

Why purpose? It turns wants into needs

So far, we have seen how purpose can give you energy, lend you focus, banish bad habits, and equip you with belief. All these are things you need to find success and fulfill your dream. But even they, on their own, are not enough.

There is one final piece in the purpose puzzle, one last gift it has to give you, and that is necessity.

This is where things get pretty simple. There are people in life who want things, and people who need things. Do I have to tell you which group reliably achieves what it sets out to do?

That's no knock on the people who want. We all want things. To be healthier. To find love. To be more financially secure. To make a difference.

But wanting is an empty feeling. It means we look but we don't touch. We think but we don't do. It's the watchword of inaction in a world where the prizes go to people who take action.

Compared to the people who want, those who need are in a different category. They give themselves no option but to act. They do because they must. Avoiding problems, delaying action, and finding excuses become alien concepts to them. They fear the consequences of not doing something and not pursuing their dream more than they do the possibility of failure. They become relentless because they give themselves no alternative.

We will all face a point in our lives when a want becomes a need, and we know what it is like to be truly motivated. Often this comes through some kind of crisis. Let's say you fall ill and see a doctor for the first time in years. They tell you some bad news: you're overweight, at risk of diabetes, and putting too much strain on your heart. Carry on like this and the consequences could be dire.

In this scenario, I can guarantee what will happen next. Having always talked about trying to be healthier, to develop a gym habit and cut out the worst parts of your diet, now you will start doing it. The broken promises to self and the failed regimes of the past become a distant memory. This time you get on one and stick to it. Because now you have a purpose—to stay alive. In the span of one doctor's appointment, your want to pursue a healthier life became an urgent need. That is the power of purpose, the force that turns wants into needs.

The same is true in business. Of all the people I have met and interviewed, I've noticed that there is a strong correlation between success and *not* starting with money. Many assume that funding is the most important ingredient for a successful business, but the reality is very different. The person with no money has to make it work and the one with money will be fine if it does not. This is the difference between wanting and needing in a nutshell. Success stems from that fundamental sense of need. A hunger that will not be satisfied unless you win.

For the same reason, having too much money can actually be a problem. I have worked with many start-ups that failed because they raised too much capital. A classic example is WeWork, which during its life raised a combined total of $22 *billion* before eventually filing for bankruptcy. Counterintuitively, if it hadn't been so well capitalized, it would have had to be more careful with the leases it signed, and had to ensure each location was a profit center not a cost center. But, because they had vast piles of investor capital, they could afford to move on sites that were never going to make a profit. Discipline was out of the window, and because money was no object, the business was built on weak foundations and wishful thinking. Even though the purpose of that business was strong, too much money helped to kill its success.

WeWork was a business where excessive funding killed the feeling of need that any company must have to succeed. Another example is Juul, the vape brand that achieved huge success before becoming mired in massive lawsuits that focused on how it had marketed its product to children. You could argue that the original purpose of the company had been strong: a product that could replace the cigarette with something far less harmful. Then Juul ran into problems and ended up having to take money from the tobacco industry, which it had set out to replace. Soon that money, the place it had come from, and the marketing campaigns it supported had destroyed the company's purpose and its reputation along with it.

That is how the decay of purpose or the suppression of need can kill a promising business. By contrast, so many successful companies are started by founders who were driven by some kind of defining life experience—a problem they *needed* to solve, a wrong in their life that they *needed* to correct. An intensely personal kind of purpose.

An entrepreneur I believe will one day meet this description is Sophie. She pitched her dream to the doorbell not long after we had set it up. The company was called I Am Denim and the idea was "tummy-friendly jeans." Sophie had become seriously ill after giving birth to her son and needed life-saving surgery from which it took some time to recover. "It was in the weeks after that I found something as simple as pulling on a pair of jeans a struggle," she said in her pitch. Her motivation was that no one else should have to go through this alone. "I could not find a pair of jeans that felt comfortable. So I created my own to help other people feel good."

Later I met Sophie and she told me how she had been struggling with her health throughout her life. She had been diagnosed with inflammatory bowel disease aged twelve, a lifelong condition that contributed to her illness after childbirth, and which in turn led to the surgery that was required to save her life. For her, this dream was a way of fighting back. "I designed these jeans with passion and to solve a problem," she said. "It's because I have been so weak at a point in my life, that being strong is a choice."

Since then her business has thrived, striking a retail partnership with Debenhams and being featured in *Vogue*. Sophie's story shows how needs can grow into purposes that power dreams. Her dream was to make a huge success of the I Am Denim brand, and the purpose that underpinned it was to ensure no one would be in the position she had been, where medical trauma was compounded by not being able to find something so simple and essential as a comfortable pair of jeans.

It reminds me of another female-founded clothing brand, the billion-dollar success story that is Spanx. Its founder, Sara Blakely, was selling fax machines door-to-door when she became frustrated by how all the underwear she bought was visible through her clothing. She knew there must be a better way, but she scoured the market and couldn't find anyone who was selling what she wanted to buy. So she created it herself in the form of shapewear. She built a massive business based on this, and as a result became the youngest female billionaire in America. Her need produced a dream, one that was kept afloat with the express purpose of elevating women.

All her success stemmed from purpose—being in a situation where she didn't just want to build the business and invent the product; she *needed* to. It wasn't a choice but a compulsion. At this point, it doesn't matter that you are up against established giants, that the unit economics don't appear to work, the supply chain is tricky, and nobody has ever tried this before.

It's personal, it's a necessity, and more often than not it will happen.

These two things—a purpose that grows out of a fundamental need—are a superpower in life. They are a form of invincibility against setbacks, adversity, and competitors. People can copy you and try to clone your business model, but they can't match your purpose, your hunger, and your risk appetite. They can't replicate your compulsive sense of need. They will lose because they lack the most important asset you have. That is the beauty of purpose. A person can't borrow it and an AI can't simulate it. It can't be passed down from one generation to the next. The government can't tax it and investors can't buy it (unless you choose to take their money). Your purpose is the one asset that you will always have whatever else you lose.

Look after your purpose and it will, I promise, pay you back over and over. Nurturing it is one of the best investments you will ever make.

Hopefully by this point I've convinced you that a dream in your life is necessary, and how you need a purpose (or several) to achieve it. Perhaps you've started to detach yourself from those old myths about hard work being the answer to your problems, or failure being the thing to avoid. You may already have a clear dream in your head, ready to press the doorbell and pitch, or you might just be waking up to the importance of having one.

Whatever the case, I can almost guarantee that somewhere you are stuck. You might have the idea and not be sure how to start it or take it to the next level. You might be holding on to a dream that you have never admitted to a living soul. You might be scared that someone is going to steal your dream or get there first (I'll talk later about why this is a groundless fear). Or you might be struggling to see what a dream means for you, and how you will discover yours.

The first thing to know is this is normal. Everyone needs help and everyone gets stuck at one point or another. The important thing is to be honest about it and to recognize exactly where you are. Understand that and the solution—that all-important next step—becomes simple. So let me give you a helping hand.

In this next chapter, I want to introduce you to the staircase: my summary of all the places people get stuck when trying to pursue a dream—every blocker and limiting belief I hear when I talk to people about this. Standing on its steps are people ranging from those who are reluctant to embrace a dream to others who feel trapped by their financial situation, or are afraid because they have chased a dream before and been disappointed. My purpose is to show you the main points at which people get stuck, and how to overcome them. Once you know which step you are standing on, and how to climb beyond it, then you will be truly ready to define, pursue, and start achieving your dream.

4.

Seven Steps

People pass us by in life. Especially today, when most of us walk around with our earphones in, heads down, and cut off from the world. On your daily commute or walk to the gym, you might pass half a dozen people who could change your life and you'd never know.

That's what almost happened to Sam, who I met in Hong Kong. She was striding down the street so fast that she could have been jogging, a huge bottle of water in one hand and a pastry in a paper bag in the other. It turned out that she was on her way to a date. But first I had a question for her. *The* question.

She didn't have to think twice.

"Yeah, I have a dream. I want to have my own catering business."

I love it when this happens. When I pose the question to someone who could say literally anything, and they come straight out with it. *Yes*, they have a dream. *Yes*, they have been thinking about it for a long time. *Yes*, they know what business they want to start, what people they want to help, even what it is going to be called.

"What's stopping you doing it?"

The second question. In many ways, the hard one.

"I don't know how to start a business. And it's just a dream."

It's just a dream. A few words that left many more unspoken:

I'll never do it.

It won't happen.

It's difficult.

I can't.

I'm afraid to try.

I had met Sam only seconds earlier, but I already knew she was in the situation so many people find themselves in. She had a dream—a very achievable one. She had the necessary skills, as we would very soon find out. She even had a name for the business she was afraid to start: Chez Sam. And I always tell people that once you have named it, you can launch it.

There was nothing stopping Sam from pursuing that dream. Nothing, that is, except herself.

This is a self-destructive tendency that so many of us have. The voice in our head that says we don't have the ability, and we can't do it because we don't know how. This is a lie, because for most things it's *easy* to find out how. All the world's knowledge is available at the touch of a button. When we say we don't have the ability, or the experience, what we really mean is that we don't have the courage.

I knew that Sam, like thousands if not millions of other people, was at a crucial juncture in her life. Our chance meeting had happened at just the right moment. If she didn't do anything with this dream, then that doubting voice would get louder. The belief that she didn't know how to do it would become stronger. So strong that it would soon be inescapable.

This is a tough truth about our dreams. They don't stay fresh forever. If we keep denying them and telling ourselves they are out of reach, then we will make that a reality. Like a ripe piece of fruit, they need to be picked or they are destined to go rotten.

Our conversation was timely, because Sam couldn't let this

idea hang around forever, and also because I was only in town for a week. Days later we would launch HelpBnk in Hong Kong to an audience of influential entrepreneurs. I immediately saw that my launch event could also become Sam's, if she was up for it.

If she could bring some samples of her food, she would be pitching her concept to a room full of people with the ability to become both customers and investors. Every single one of them was a business owner who at some stage would be running events. Most of them were investors. We couldn't have planned a better launchpad if we had tried. So, would she do it? Would she bring some of her food to the HelpBnk launch and take the first step to making Chez Sam a reality?

Sam said yes, OK. But in truth she sounded a little noncommittal. "I've really got to run," she said. She had that date to get to. I had given her the time and the place to turn up, and I had tried to sell her on the opportunity. While I was desperately hoping she would show up, if I'm being honest, I wasn't sure. Nor were plenty of people in the comments when I posted the video on TikTok. "Bro is not coming." "She won't do it." "She's not serious."

Three days later, the night of the launch arrived. I'd had no further contact with Sam. Either she was about to walk through the door or I would never see her again. I had those butterflies you get when a part of you worries you are going to be stood up.

Then the door opened and all my doubts melted away. It was Sam, dressed to impress and with a tray of baked goods under her arm. When I had first met her, she was carrying a croissant she had bought from someone else's shop. Now, just seventy-two hours later, she had made her own delicacies and was catering her first event. More than that, she was pitching

73

the business she had doubted she could launch to an audience of experts, and doing it brilliantly. "I'm going to grab the chance, I'm going to show people my food," she told them. Chez Sam had been born. Hong Kong's newest entrepreneur had arrived. And it had all happened by chance, in the course of a few days. The buzz created by Sam's video meant it was viewed by over 17 million people on TikTok alone, and we gave her the revenue from the video as seed funding for her business.

I am sharing Sam's story not just because it is an example of what is possible, but because it could so easily have turned out differently. What if no one had given her that nudge, saying that they believed in her and wanted to become her first customer? Would she have gotten the business started? There is no way of knowing.

What I *do* know is that Sam is representative of so many other people: walking around with a plan in their head but without either the confidence or the impetus to pursue it. People who aren't doing anything about their dreams, and who risk seeing them grow old and die. People who are stuck.

I sometimes get comments on my TikToks with a three-letter acronym: NPC. This originates in video games, where it means nonplayable character, one of the background figures who you might meet and talk to during the game. It's been adopted as slang for people who are going through their lives in exactly this kind of preprogrammed way. Without freedom, without direction, and without a dream. NPC-dom is what we are all trying to avoid. To do that, we need to work out what's blocking us.

You might be stuck at the same stage as Sam, or at an earlier or later point on the journey. But the advice is the same at all stages. If you want to get moving, then you need to work out what's holding you back. What combination of doubts, limiting beliefs, life circumstances, and social conditioning is stopping you from pursuing your idea, and starting on it right now. This is where the journey towards discovering and pursuing *your* dream really begins.

Let me help you speed up the process. In this chapter, I'm going to give you the cheat codes: all the reasons people give for not pursuing their dreams, and all the reasons these are wrong. How you can bust through your limiting beliefs to awaken your purpose and unlock your dream.

To do that, we have to climb a staircase, one made up of all the excuses that people give for why their dream isn't possible. There are only seven steps, but each of them is a potential dream killer until you learn how to recognize and overcome it. You might be starting this journey from the bottom step or near the top, but before you can pursue your dream, first you need to put all these blockers behind you. So let's work out where you are currently standing, and climb the steps together.

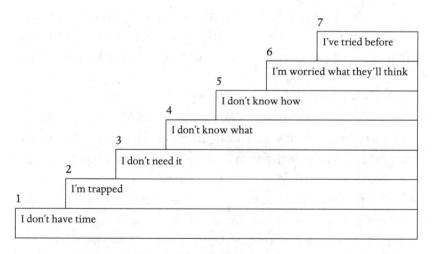

7 — I've tried before
6 — I'm worried what they'll think
5 — I don't know how
4 — I don't know what
3 — I don't need it
2 — I'm trapped
1 — I don't have time

The Seven Steps

Step 1: I don't have time

Some of the people I approach with my microphone don't even try to answer the question. They brush me off, shake their heads, or give me that smile that says they think it's all a bit ridiculous.

If I can get a person like this to stop and talk to me, they will probably say one of the following things.

I've got bills to pay.

I've got a job.

I don't have time.

Or, my favorite one ever: "I'm trying to catch this bus."

If you're in this situation, then a dream isn't even on the table. You haven't allowed yourself to think about it. The idea of a dream isn't just outlandish, but almost offensive. When your life is already so full of obligations, and makes so many demands on your time, it feels frivolous. It's practically an insult to your hard work to suggest that there could and should be something more.

If this comes even close to describing you, then let me tell you the problem. You are in survival mode. A way of living that is based on getting through the day, getting to the weekend, and making it through to the end of the month.

And I understand. I get it. There have been times in my life when I had no money and could think of nothing except where the next bit of work was coming from, and how to put food on my table. I know what it means to struggle and to think that there can be nothing more than survival.

The problem isn't being in survival mode; it's accepting it. Believing that this is your life and there is nothing you can or should do about it. If that is your mindset, then I promise you nothing is going to change. You have set the limits of your life and you will live within them. You are trapped and you won't escape.

That is why the journey towards a dream must begin with ditching ideas like "I don't have time" and "it's not for me." **These things are only true if you let them be.** Accepting a dream, allowing yourself permission to think about it, is your ticket out of this prison.

Why? Because when you make space for your dream and acknowledge it, your mindset changes in an instant. You start thinking about the future and imagining something better. Soon you are taking your first step towards it. It might be a tiny tiptoe and that is fine: at the start distance doesn't matter, only direction. You are moving forward, even if it is slowly and in your spare time.

You spend one minute a day thinking about it, and then five minutes. You start to make notes, to doodle ideas, even to talk to people about it. If the dream is real, then before long you won't be able to stop thinking about it. That is the power of the dream, how what begins as a barely perceptible spark can be nourished into a roaring blaze. And it's why one of the most powerful blockers is the idea that the dream isn't possible. Remove that and you will be amazed how quickly things can start to change. Your mindset has shifted, and now everything has become possible.

Step 2: I'm trapped

When I offer to help someone with their dream, whether by giving them money, connecting them to people, or profiling them on my channels, I never know how it will end. The people I meet and offer to work with are strangers to me, as I am to them.

Twice on this journey I have worked with people where the outcome was not good. These stories ended up more or less the same way, and I believe it was for the same reason—the same blocker that many people will face as we chase our dreams.

In 2022, I met Davide. A young chef from Italy, he had been dreaming since he was a child of owning his own restaurant. He was confident and charismatic as he explained his concept: The Black Pearl. I believed in him. So did many of the 30 million people who viewed his video. Occasionally I get a really good feeling about the people I meet—their dreams seem so clear, so deeply felt, that I am almost certain they will gain traction. With Davide, that feeling was as strong as it had ever been. On a gorgeous sunny day, in the shadow of Big Ben, meeting him felt like destiny.

I didn't just want to give Davide a nudge in the right direction. I was desperate to see this restaurant dream become the reality it deserved to be. I followed his story, arranged for him to cook what turned out to be a wonderful meal for a gathered group of hospitality and restaurant experts, and helped him raise more than $13,000 online. We helped him get a trademark for the name—remarkably, given its association with a popular movie. I thought everything was on track.

Then Davide disappeared. Months passed with no updates and messages going unanswered. Eventually, it emerged that he had gone home to Italy. He had debts, heavy ones, and had decided it was better to start paying these off before opening the restaurant. The restaurant I had been convinced he was going to launch would not open its doors—at least not for now.

I felt sad and concerned for Davide. I wished he had told me about his past financial problems, but I think he was ashamed of them. I still get asked about his story and believe that he may fulfill that dream—one that inspired so many people to support him. But his story had shown how the problems we run away from can come back to haunt us if we refuse to confront them. How they can be a trap that even the strongest dream will not help us to escape.

The tough reality is we cannot achieve our dreams without first confronting our problems. The very things we tend to ignore or try to sweep under the carpet are the exact ones that will kill our dreams unless we deal with them. Often we are ashamed of these things when they are not in fact our fault. And we make the situation worse by not being honest, with ourselves and other people, or by turning away those who try to help us. We deepen the hole we are in by turning away the people who are trying to get us out.

If you want to have a dream, then my advice is to start with complete honesty and clean the slate. Be transparent about the problems in your life and have the humility to admit if you need help or support. Don't assume that you can stuff your problems away in a cupboard or ignore them. I promise you that every unresolved issue you store up now is one that will hurt you later.

Step 3: I don't need it

"That's not for me."

I often get this response from people who say they are happy with what they have. They have a job; maybe they've bought a house and are eyeing up their next car. They are happy—or at least that's what they tell themselves and anyone who asks.

Scratch the surface and there is a different story. The house is mostly mortgaged. The car is financed. Whether they like their job or not, they are stuck in it.

This is a different kind of trap: one where we create a prison of our own financial obligations. Debt and repayments control us. The air gets squeezed out of our dreams.

This is where the urge for possessions I described earlier can lead. All the things you thought you wanted end up owning you. You aren't working to achieve your dream, but to pay back the money you owe.

People who are trapped like this may say they don't "need" a dream, but that is a cover story. The truth is that they can't have one and they know it. All the things they really wanted to achieve have become buried under a pile of bills and a stack of obligations.

I don't trust people who say that a dream isn't necessary or important to them. Those who are winning at life will tell you that they are already living their dream, and offer to share their hard-won wisdom. Whereas people who deny a dream are usually expressing a sense of frustration that their life is being dominated by their finances.

I think the majority of people are stuck on this step. They have let their dream die and blamed their obligations in life. They say they're living like this for their kids, and that's true. Here's the problem with that: **kids don't do what you say, they do what you do**. If the example you set them is of someone who stays in a job they hate just to pay the mortgage, there is a very good chance that this is the life they will have themselves, twenty or thirty years from now. As parents, we want our kids to have dreams. To have exciting and fulfilling lives. Too many of us think the way to achieve that is to deny our own dreams. That's what a lot of people are really saying when they tell me that they "don't need" a dream.

The good news is you can escape this trap. It won't be easy

because the only solution to debt is that you have to pay it back and the only recourse for lifestyle overreach is to get your costs down by any means necessary. You will need to be ruthless and give up some things you have gotten used to. You might need to sell the car that you convinced yourself you could afford, or think about moving into a home with a smaller mortgage to help you free up some cash. If you're lucky enough to be young and without major financial obligations, then the only thing you need to change is your mindset: stop thinking about the next watch you are going to buy, or daydreaming about making big money trading crypto, and start focusing on a real dream.

To climb this step, you have to renounce your belief in possessions as the end goal in life. It's a difficult but also tremendously liberating thing, like losing weight. You will literally feel lighter as a result. The mental space for a dream will become available to you.

Living within your means doesn't make you unambitious, just as a flash car or watch bought on credit doesn't make you wealthy or successful. It's actually one of the most powerful things you can do. It will allow you to live without fearing the bill that lands at the end of the month, and to gain the freedom to have a dream. There is no possession in the world that can be as valuable as that.

Step 4: I don't know what

"I don't know."

I have never quantified the responses people give when I ask them what their dream is, but this one would be near the top of the list. It's our default response when someone asks a difficult question: we try to shut it down, to avoid doing the hard work of thinking about our answer.

This is a different limitation from saying "I don't have time" or "I don't need it." The person who says they don't know is not *rejecting* the idea of a dream. They just haven't properly engaged with it yet. They are open to it, and that is a good start.

The remarkable thing about people in this situation is that a dream is usually there, pretty close to the surface. It doesn't take a huge amount of digging to unearth it. If I can get them to stop and talk, then I will ask more questions: what do they do for a living, what do they like about it, what would they be doing if money was no object?

Of course, it's possible that your dream is something completely outside your current life experience. You might be longing to travel the world because you've hardly ever left this country, or to make music even if you've never tried before.

But for many of us, the dream is closer than that. It's related to something that's already in our life. A different and better version of what we are already doing. You might work as a server and want to open your own restaurant. Perhaps you play in a band on weekends and really want to start your own music business.

Kellie, who we met earlier, was a great example. She was working as a dog groomer, the only thing she wanted to do, but she wasn't happy. She knew it could be done better and she needed the freedom to work with animals the way she wanted. For her it was simple: she had to start her own business.

She knew her dream, but the people stuck on this step

don't. They have the impulse to do something different but have never really articulated it. They have a lingering dissatisfaction with their routine, a pebble in their shoe they walk around with every day at work, but they don't do anything about it.

That is where the idea of a dream can be so helpful. It requires you to think hard about what you do and don't want in life. It makes you confront those things that limit and hold you back and it focuses you on what your perfect idea of life could look like.

A lot of people never do this until they are forced to. I once met a successful entrepreneur who had never thought about starting his own business before he was laid off from the company where he had worked his whole career. He had given them twenty years' service, but they used a technicality to avoid awarding him any severance pay. At the time, he was distraught, but it turned out to be the best day of his life. Call it anger, revenge, even fate, but now he had his dream. He would start his own company and he would do it better than the people who had deemed him disposable. By the time he was done, his own business was five times the size of the one that had laid him off.

I guarantee that if I'd met this man while he was still in his original job, and asked him about his dream, he'd have said he wasn't sure he had one. That's why the people who "don't know" are almost always lying to themselves. They do know actually, if they only stopped to think. To ask themselves what they really like doing, what they most enjoy about their life or work, and how they can spend more of their time doing that, and less on the things they secretly hate.

If your gut response to the title of this book is that you're "not sure" or "don't know," then do yourself a favor. Ban those phrases and make yourself answer the question again. Start writing out a list of likes and dislikes. That will lead you to your strengths and weaknesses, the hobbies that you could maybe turn into a career, and the way you really want to spend your time. Before long you will be thinking about practicalities: the things you can do for yourself, and others you need help with. Where and how to start. Soon you will not just have worked out your dream—you'll be working out how to achieve it too.

Step 5: I don't know how

The early steps are made up of people who say they don't have a dream. They don't have time. Don't need it. Haven't thought about it.

For lots of people, none of these things are true. They have a dream and have been thinking about it for some time. They can put a name on it and they can imagine it. When I ask them, often they come straight out with it (though some treat it like a guilty secret: one woman working in a luxury goods shop first said that she didn't want to be interviewed, and then almost whispered to me that her dream was to be an artist, as if worried someone might overhear).

What is blocking these people who don't deny a dream is possible and already know what theirs is? To put it simply, they are afraid and they are overthinking it.

This is where, as human beings, we can be our own worst enemies. Our brains are in some ways too complex and too capable. Rather than rushing straight towards the thing that

84

instinct is telling us to do, we think about it. We stop and ask ourselves if it's wise. If it's feasible. If we are good enough. We create artificial barriers by saying that we don't have the right credentials, qualifications, or experience.

Soon that old fear of failure has kicked in and we decide not to try. The dream goes on a shelf and it sits there. Quite possibly, it never leaves.

This is exactly the situation that Sam was in when I ran into her in Hong Kong. She had a plan so well developed that she could put a name on it, but hadn't done anything about it. She knew what she wanted the business to be called, but doubted her ability to get it off the ground. She was stuck in a circle that she might have kept walking round and round forever.

Her story was a great example of how irrational these fears are. Within days, she had done her first catering event. She had the skill, the will, and the ideas to make it work. All she had been missing was the belief.

The truth is that most of us underestimate ourselves and we overestimate the world. We assume that everything we want to achieve is incredibly difficult and that the people doing it must be geniuses whose abilities far exceed our own. This is nonsense: a self-fulfilling prophecy that guarantees you will never get anything done.

Of course there are things in life that are incredibly difficult and reserved for a select few. Not many of us will become an Olympic athlete, have a chart-topping album, or win the Academy Award for best actor or director.

But those are, for most of us, daydreams rather than real dreams. And it is real dreams—*achievable* ones—that most people tell me about. To open a restaurant, launch a clothing brand, become a photographer, make art or music. These are things that hundreds of thousands of people do around the world every day. The bar is much lower than we think for peo-ple with dedication, belief, and the willingness to learn. But we instinctively disbelieve this: we assume it must be incredibly hard and we allow that belief to grow and grow. Rather than breaking the dream down into a series of things we can achieve and start doing right now, we build up our objections and doubts until they tower above us. We put so much effort into convincing ourselves it will be difficult that, eventually, we are almost forced to believe it.

Lots of people are stuck on this step. They know their dream. It might only be drawn in broad strokes, it might be a guilty secret, but they know what it looks like. They can imag-ine that future. The problem is that they run away from it and not towards it.

If this describes you, then my first piece of advice is to stop. No longer permit yourself to say that you don't know, you're not sure, or it might be too hard. Instead, focus on what you can do. Write a list of achievable actions that will move you closer to your goal—and start doing them. Work out where you want to be a week, a month, and a year from now. Chart the path and begin to walk it.

This is what I do when I meet people who have a dream but say they are wavering about whether to do it, and don't know if it's possible. I keep asking them questions that make the idea more tangible: What's the business called? When can you do a demo for me? How much do you charge? and How much money do you need to get started? You can do the same thing for yourself: stop pondering big-picture problems and start posing yourself specific questions that lead you to actions. Shrink the size of the problem until you feel confi-dent in taking the next step.

I promise that once you are *doing* things rather than *thinking* about them, the doubts will start to fall away. You will realize that most of your fears were unfounded. Now you are beginning to live the dream that you thought only yesterday wasn't possible. Take those first steps and you will start to see how much you can really achieve.

Step 6: I'm worried what they'll think

When I think about the difference between dreams that are achieved and those that go unfulfilled, I think about Charlie, who I knew when we were in our twenties. He had become a bus driver, but one evening told me his real love was drawing. After some prompting, he got out a pen, opened out a paper napkin on the table in front of us, and did a thirty-second doodle. I am no artist, but I could tell immediately that he had a huge talent. Like so many brilliant people, he presented his genius with a shrug. He batted away my compliments and shook his head when I told him that he was so talented that he should make this his career.

Soon the reason emerged. Charlie's belief in himself, which was not that strong to begin with, was being further undermined by his partner. She had kept telling him that he needed to get a proper job, which is how he had ended up driving. Every time he tried to put together a portfolio of work and get commissioned by a magazine or book publisher, she would say that it was the wrong time, or probably wouldn't lead to anything.

In the end, Charlie overcame both of their doubts and got a contract with one of the leading children's publishers. He stopped driving and became a successful artist. But it had taken years longer than it should have, and even then I believe he was one of the lucky ones. His experience was a common one, and often the outcome goes the other way: a person gives up on their dreams because those closest to them were not supportive.

This happens more than you might think. We tell our parents, our partners, and our friends about the big idea. We say we are thinking about quitting our job and going all in. Often the response comes back in a single word: *don't*. Or perhaps in three words: *are you sure?*

The impact of such doubt can be profound. Hearing someone question your dream can kill your confidence stone dead. At worst, it can reawaken old concerns that you may have previously put to rest. Especially so when it comes from a family member, a partner, or a close friend. Someone who knows us and wants the best for us. When people like this express doubt, it magnifies our own.

The problem is that they have no better chance of being right than you do. If they are questioning your dream, telling you it is unrealistic, or worrying that it might all go wrong, they are probably not speaking from a position of expertise but one of fear. You may be trying to do something that goes well beyond their life experience. A parent who has worked their whole life in a corporate job may naturally feel uncomfortable if their child says that they want to be self-employed. People who are lawyers, accountants, and bankers doubt how anyone can make money as an artist or in the music industry.

These are influential people and voices in our life, and they can easily wreck a dream in its early stages, when it is at its most fragile—just an idea that exists in your head, with no verifiable proof that it will work. This is the hardest time to be confident and the easiest one to be critical.

It means you have to be ready for people who will try to dissuade you, often with good intentions. If this happens, then don't take it to heart. Rationalize it. Ask yourself why they are saying it. Use this to decide if you should take the warnings seriously or not. Consider if they have really said something that you haven't yet thought about, or provided new information.

Above all, do not let yourself be easily dissuaded. Don't let someone else's fears become your own (and, as a general rule of thumb, only take advice from people if you want a life like theirs; if you don't want their life, don't take their advice). If you truly believe in your dream when you start to share it with other people, then you should keep believing even when others doubt. Don't become one of those people who surrendered their dream to the first critic.

Step 7: I've tried before

Once you have gotten past other people's doubts, there is just one more step to climb. The hurdle of past experience.

People who have tried and failed can be some of the hardest to convince that a dream is possible. They are once bitten, twice shy, and have told themselves that they are never going through that again.

This is an irrational response to failure that deprives us of its most important lessons.

As someone who has run nineteen businesses, I know this to be true. A few succeeded but plenty failed. Some failed before they had really gotten off the ground, and others after years of effort. One cost me more than a million dollars.

But I'm grateful for those failures. Each of them taught me something and made me a better entrepreneur. Sometimes, as with *DevaShard*, they saved me from things that would have looked like success at the time but caused problems later.

That's why it frustrates me when people use their experience as a barrier. When they say that it didn't work the first time, so they are not trying again. This turns everything we know about how to succeed on its head. It's like trying to read this book backwards and turned upside down. Or if Usain Bolt had given up on sprinting because he didn't set a world record on his first go.

People in this situation have what I call bad fear. They have let the fear stop them from trying, because they haven't diagnosed its source or rationalized their feelings. The untreated fear—of failing, of being judged, of missing out, or not meeting expectations—has become bigger than the dream, and they have given up. Unlike good fear, which acts as a motivation to be and do your best, bad fear is overwhelming and debilitating. Good fear is the friend who holds you accountable for going to the gym with them three times a week, or the friends who I enlisted as investors in HelpBnk, because I knew I wouldn't want to let them down, and that the fear of doing so would help to drive me. Bad fear is an enemy, and often one that stems from past experience.

It's completely natural to have fears when you set out on a big project and to feel dejected when we encounter failure. Even after years of running businesses, experiencing both success and failure, these things still happen to me. I've felt the fear of failure while writing this book: worrying that it will not be good enough, that people won't enjoy it, or that it won't sell. Not long ago, I gave a TED talk, which I spent weeks worrying about—a fear which I slowly calmed through meticulous preparation.

The problem is not *experiencing* those feelings, but being *controlled* by them. A little bit of fear can sharpen us up and help us perform at our best, but too much (when we haven't broken down our worries and rationalized them) becomes overwhelming. A dose of anger and embarrassment when we fail is fine, driving us on to do better, but if those feelings linger then you become bitter rather than motivated. You give up on your dream rather than picking yourself up to have another go.

This is where people on the seventh step are stuck. They have "bad fear" about history repeating itself. They think that past failures prove they aren't capable, and that giving up is the right thing to do. In fact, the opposite is true. Those failures will make you stronger if you allow them to. That experience, which feels like a millstone, can become an asset if you approach it with the right mindset.

The first thing to do is to take the failure out of the box you have locked it in. Stop treating it as a place you must never return to and allow yourself to reflect. What went wrong and why? Was it the wrong idea, the wrong time in your life, or the wrong people you chose to partner with? Did circumstances conspire against you and were you just unlucky? If you look for the real answers, it's very likely that the story is more complicated than the one you've been telling yourself. You didn't fail because you are useless or incompetent. You failed because of bad decisions, or unfortunate timing, or a lack of discipline in certain areas. Mostly things that you could do better the second or third time around.

The next thing you must do is forgive yourself for the failure. Stop beating yourself up about what happened. Unless you leave behind your emotions, you will never be able to analyze those events objectively and learn from them.

This is something that I was taught by Adam, one of my cofounders at HelpBnk. He'd had a career in the music industry that had begun at the age of thirteen, when he'd released records with major labels as well as writing numerous hit singles. But as he told me, he had been burned on multiple occasions by people who didn't pay him what they had promised or honor contract terms.

When we had been working on HelpBnk for some time without a formal agreement in place, I asked him why he wasn't asking for us to nail down terms. Hadn't his past experiences made him less trusting? His response was that he was in some ways grateful for all the times he had been screwed over in the past. Rather than making him suspicious of everyone, it had taught him that the most important decision in business is choosing who to trust. Far better to be working with people you can trust totally than in situations where you are left relying on the terms of a contract, which may not protect you as well as you'd hoped.

This is a great example of how to process and overcome the failures or setbacks of the past; how to use them as lessons rather than sticks to beat ourselves with. Adam didn't let his bad experiences of business get in the way of what he wanted to do now. He had turned what could have been a weakness into a strength—leaving himself free to continue pursuing his ambitions, and better equipped than he would have been otherwise. He was using past experiences as a source of strength, something we must all learn to do if we are going to remove the barriers standing between us and our dreams.

———

So, have you located the step you are currently on? Are you one of those people who has never thought about a dream before, or are you walking around with a big idea that you haven't ever talked about? Well, this is the time to admit it, to write it down, and to be honest about what is holding you back. You need to clear these barriers out of the way to give yourself the best chance at success. And you need to do it now, because we are about to turn our attention to *your* dream. What is it, how will you define it, and how can we achieve it together?

PART TWO

Your Dream

How to unlock, discover, and define your dream

5.

Three Questions

Where do I start? It's probably the question you're asking your-self now. It's a question some people spend their whole lives thinking about.

You might be wondering how to start working towards a dream you have already defined, or how to get to the point where you know your dream in the first place. For now, I am going to assume you're in the second camp and start from the beginning. Even if you have your dream in mind, I recommend you go through these steps as an exercise, to kick the tires and make sure you are heading in the right direction. And if you don't yet know your dream, then what I set out here is going to help you find it.

So, where do you start? It's often said that nothing in life is more intimidating than a blank page. When you could say, think, or write absolutely anything, how could you possibly know where to begin?

That might be true for novelists or film writers, but it isn't for most of us. Because there is no blank page in life. Not for me, not for you, not for anyone. Our pages are already covered in notes, doodles, corrections, and bits we've crossed out. We have a whole lifetime that has shaped us, given us good and bad experiences, and provided insight into ourselves and the world. All of us have been molded by the places we grew up in, the people who raised us, and those we have spent our lives learning, working, and hanging out with.

This conditioning is a part of us, whether we like it or not. We can lament this, complaining that we are the prisoner of the life we were born into. Or we can use it.

All the things that have happened to us in life are in some way significant. If we examine them properly and learn from them, we can discover remarkable things. Within our life history, we will find the basis for everything that matters: our outlook on the world, our motivations, our pain, and our sense of self and purpose.

That's why I think **the question of where to start is actually the easy bit**. Although it seems difficult, in fact we already have the answers. They are right there, buried in different areas of our life experience. We can quickly find them if we know how and where to look.

It's also why I believe the path to the future—towards the dream—begins by looking back. Not to wallow in the past or to feel nostalgia or regret, but to really understand ourselves and our lives. To ask the questions that will reveal who we are, what we want, and what we cannot live without. These are the three questions that I will set out in this chapter. Once you can answer these, I promise that you will be ready to articulate your dream—maybe even to say it out loud.

Question #1: *What are my likes and dislikes?*

When I was forty-two, in that slightly listless phase of my life where I had sold my business and didn't know what to do next, "Where do I start?" was the question I asked myself.

I was beginning to think about what it meant to have a

dream, and why I'd never thought about this before. I'd been so busy building the business that I had never looked back on my life and really reflected on it. Now, I finally had the chance.

As I did this, I stumbled upon what I now know is the first key question in working out your dream. A simple question.

What do I like doing?

. Knowing the answer to this might seem obvious. Because surely everyone knows what they like, and tries to organize their life to allow them to do more of it? Don't they?

I wish this was true, *but it isn't*. The truth is that many of us turn this common sense on its head. **We spend most of our lives doing something we don't really enjoy and relegate the things we love into small corners of spare time.** We treat our passions as hobbies and our interests as incidental.

I am shocked by the number of people who believe they can't or shouldn't build their lives around the things they are good at and love to do. This self-defeating attitude is perhaps another hangover from school, when we were told to focus our efforts on the subjects we were weakest at, rather than being brilliant at the ones we could do well. This training encouraged us to believe that life should be hard and that we should fear our weaknesses more than we believe in our strengths. It shaped a worldview that affects so many of us, in which we believe that our passions are not serious and do not deserve to be taken seriously.

Pursuing a dream means banishing this philosophy and thinking—perhaps for the first time—about what you really like. You need to be completely honest with yourself: what do you really love to do? What are you really good at? What is important to you? Write down the actual answers, not the ones you wish were true or you think will impress other people. Tell the truth!

Here is how that process went for me. What my list of likes and dislikes looked like.

I liked meeting people and talking to them, helping entrepreneurs with their businesses, selling stuff, and sharing what I have learned. I didn't like sitting in meetings, working with difficult people, poring over numbers, reading long documents, or—as I had discovered—having nothing to do.

In fact, having nothing to do was the worst possible thing for me, because it is people that give me energy. Like a lot of people who retire early, I'd discovered that you can have too much time on your hands, and there's nothing worse than being someone who *used to be* busy. Which is exactly why retirement is a fake dream, designed to keep us working through our prime years for the promise of a future that often turns out to be disappointing. Far better to pursue your real dream while you still have your best years ahead of you.

Having nothing to do made me realize how much I needed the energy and buzz of a business to run and people to be around. If I spend hours talking to someone, brainstorming ideas, and sharing problems, I will feel more energized at the end than I did at the beginning. Whereas if I spend that time playing golf, I'll be tired by the end, because I feel like nothing has been achieved except maybe to shave a bit off my handicap.

We all have these dividing lines in our personality and unique makeup. Things we like and don't like. Things that give us energy and others that drain it. Things you are good at and those you struggle with.

Knowing these things gives you the raw material for your dream. The building blocks. In my case, piecing my dream together began with several of the "likes" on my list. I wanted to be able to talk to people, to share ideas, and in some way or form to teach. So I started a podcast and spent the next year interviewing 200 entrepreneurs about their businesses, their lives, and their paths to success. I wanted to know how other people had done it and how their journeys compared to my own. For want of a better word, I was being a bit nosy.

I had no idea how to manage or promote a podcast. My equipment was terrible and I wasn't an experienced interviewer. In fact, I deliberately started it on the cheap. In 2019, Helen bought me a $130 microphone as a present and I started using it. I enjoyed the low-cost, bootstrapping vibe: I didn't want to invest the thousands I could have afforded into something I wasn't yet sure would be a long-term project.

When I listen back to some of those old episodes now, I cringe, but I loved making them at the time. I was doing exactly what I needed and wanted to be doing. Having interesting conversations. Getting beyond my own survival bias about what it takes to succeed in business. Beginning to build a community on social media. However uncertain, it was the beginning of everything I do today: promoting the idea of a better world in which we all help one another, in which networks and knowledge are shared equally among us all. It led me towards my dream. This crappy, low-budget podcast was actually one of the most important things I have done, and I did it the same way I say everyone can start a business—with a cheap bit of kit I got for Christmas.

Soon, I was experimenting with different content formats, finding new ways to reach and build my audience. I realized that I'd had the right idea, but in slightly the wrong direction. I didn't just want to kick back and shoot the breeze with people who had already made it (though it took me 200 episodes to realize this).

Instead, I wanted to work with people who were still trying

to make it. I wanted to help people who really needed it, just like I had when starting my first business at fifteen. Over time, this purpose led to my videos on TikTok, and everything else I have done to try and support people to achieve their dreams.

That is why the first question is about your likes and dislikes. You might not yet have a fixed dream or purpose, but if you start with something you like doing, then you can be almost certain that you are moving in the right direction. It might take a few goes, but you will get there.

Another approach is to ask yourself: what would you do today if you didn't have to go to work or worry about getting paid? If you had all the freedom in the world, what would you be doing right now? That is your starting point. Don't fear taking money out of the equation to start with: we will get to that and how to create a business model around your passion. At the beginning, the important thing is that you are starting with something you really care about. That is how you guarantee the dream will be durable.

A lot of people don't agree with me on this point, about the importance of rooting your dream (and the business you will build around it) in something you love. Start with a market gap or something that no one else is doing, they say. Find a problem you can solve. Think about what other people want. They are wrong. Why? **Because it's never the idea that makes a business succeed. It's the people and the motivation behind it—the dream that powers it.** If you have this, then you can work forever without feeling like it's work. You will push on through inevitable failures and persist when others give up. That kind of focus and desire doesn't come from trying to fill a gap in the market, but from pursuing something that is important and life-defining to you. Unless your dream is rooted in something you really care about and love doing, it is very likely going to fail.

I know this because I have seen time and time again what happens when people start businesses without a deep personal commitment. One company I invested in was meant to be the Asian equivalent of Red Letter Days, allowing people to give experiences as gifts. Its founder approached me with a simple pitch: "It's a successful business in Europe and it's not been done in Asia yet." He had all the figures to back him up—market size, revenue potential, demographics. I invested because it looked like a robust business plan. But I had made a rookie error: I didn't ask him *why* this idea mattered to him. Of all the business ideas in the world, why had he landed on this one?

I realized this mistake after the business failed and we ended up selling what was left to one of its main competitors. Their business was succeeding while ours was floundering, and I wanted to know why. When I spent some time with the founder, the answer soon became clear. Her pitch was a hundred times more compelling than the one I had invested in a few years before. "I want people to spend their money on having experiences, not things—my family spent money on things for me when I was younger and I just wanted experiences and time with them," she said. This founder was not just creating an opportunistic copycat company. She was building a business with a mission that she believed in and that was rooted in her life experience. That alone explained why she had won. It's why I have come to believe that there is no such thing as a special idea in business, only a special ability to execute on it. Almost always, you find that ability when someone is building a business that is grounded in a dream.

This is why I am urging you to take seriously the question of what you like and dislike. To think about what your passion and purpose in life really are.

"What do I like to do?" may sound like a simplistic question, and it is meant to. It frees your mind from all the clutter and complication and focuses you on something real. It's a question that all of us can answer *right now*, because there is not a person alive who doesn't have at least one thing they like to do, are interested in, or enjoy learning about. Perhaps you're an artist; a gamer; someone who loves to spend their weekends in the garden; whose best day of the week is the one they spend volunteering; or whose best part of the year is the time they spend traveling.

You might deny that it's possible to build your life around the things you like, you might claim that you don't have time or that other obligations are getting in the way (and we will deal with all these points later). But you can't deny that there are things you enjoy doing, things that give you energy, and things you are good at.

With these in mind, you can start taking action. Do more of the things you like, find different ways to pursue that passion, and you will learn, gather data, and hone your approach. Before long, you won't be sucking your pencil wondering what your dream is. You'll know it, because you will have bumped into it somewhere along the way. Don't worry if you can't exactly define your dream when you set out on this journey (although well done if you can). Follow the things you like doing, and they will lead you towards it.

For the vast majority of us, a dream is going to grow out of our life experiences and the things we like. We sometimes assume the dream must be some faraway notion, but in fact it is close by. Maybe you already know how to cook brilliant food, design great clothes, make music, look after animals, fix cars, or write stories. The only question is how to turn that "like" into a life: to convert it from hobby into goal, from sideline into serious business.

Does this really work? Is it really that simple? I can hear you saying, "Simon, I like to go on walks but how can that be a business?" Enter Chris, who had joined a TikTok live where I was offering $3,300 for the best business idea. He was working at a bank and his mental health had suffered so severely that he had contemplated suicide on multiple occasions. Chris recovered in part by taking to the outdoors and going on walks in the South Downs to clear his head. Now he wanted to help other people deal with the same issues he had faced.

His pitch was for a business called We Power On. The idea was simple: go on a walk, talk to each other, and at the end have a cup of tea and a biscuit. The business part was that he would make and sell his own tea and biscuits to pay for it all, turning a commodity product into a purchase with purpose. Chris's idea got the funding: I knew that with his sense of personal mission, he would do what it took to succeed. In the process, he had also demonstrated how something as simple as going for a walk can become a business. And that was just one possible business Chris could have started based on his passion. He could have started a dog-walking business, or one where he organized walking trips for paying customers. When you really start to think about it, most of our passions can be made into a business idea, and often several.

As you consider this, there is an important distinction to note. What you like and really want to do may be different from what you are already good at or have spent your career doing. Confusing the two or lying to yourself about which is which can quickly lead to trouble.

I found that out years ago, when I invested in a chef who

wanted to open his first restaurant after fifteen years of working in the industry. He said he had an idea for something no one else was doing and had the perfect venue. I liked his vision, respected his experience, and invested about $132,500 in the venture. The restaurant had a successful opening, but when I went to visit again after three months, the owner wasn't there. He was out on a photography shoot. It seemed odd, but as time went on the pattern became clear. Whenever I wanted to talk to him about the restaurant, he wanted to chat about his photography. I realized that the business he had pitched to me wasn't really the one he had wanted to run. He was tired of being a chef, and photography was his real passion. When the restaurant failed and I lost most of my investment, I said I wished he'd told me he wanted to be a photographer in the first place. I would have been happy to invest in that dream, and the outcome would probably have been better for both of us.

Like a lot of people, he was trapped by the qualifications and experience he had spent so long building. The business he felt he should be running was different from the one he really wanted to run. It was a similar story for a friend of mine who spent seven years studying to become a lawyer and then six years figuring out how to quit her legal job and start the business of her dreams. It was difficult for her because she had the "sunk cost" mentality that says you have gone so far and cannot afford to turn back now. But she did it, proving that your education and your career history don't have to trap you if you don't let them.

When you spend time thinking about your likes and dislikes, you might be surprised what you discover. Once I had settled into my routine of making videos about other people's dreams, I realized that I wasn't really doing anything new. For my whole career, I had been running one business or another that tried to help people, especially with their businesses. Fluid had been about helping brands become more successful through design. Nest, my investment business, had been about channeling funding and support to budding entrepreneurs. Now, I was basically doing the same thing, just for free and with people at a much earlier stage in their journey. I'd had this purpose all along; I just hadn't put it into words or attached it to a bigger dream.

That is the power of starting with your likes. When you don't know your destination, these passions act like a compass, making sure you are going the right way. If you keep following them, then I guarantee that you will run into your dream before long.

Question #2: What is my pain?

Knowing that I liked talking to people and wanted to help people were important parts of understanding my dream. But they weren't sufficient on their own. I also needed something that I believe is vital to almost every dream, and the purpose it contains. I needed to tap into my pain.

We've already talked about how purpose can be the product of pain—from Kellie, who turned the trauma she had suffered as a child into a motivation to care for animals, to Sophie, who was compelled by her struggles after surgery to make clothes fit for people recovering from medical trauma.

There is a very good chance that your dream and purpose will have some relation to pain. It might be your own pain or someone else's. Perhaps you are trying to prove wrong someone who doubted you, seeking to prevent others from going through the same difficult experience you did, or hoping to correct an injustice in the world.

Pain is what gives a purpose real traction—one of those forces that turns "wants" into "needs." If you really dig into the stories of most successful people, you will find pain in there somewhere: a source of motivation that comes from a deeply personal place in their lives. They might not have recognized or acknowledged it, but it is almost certainly present.

Don't get me wrong, I have seen people succeed without pain in their lives. But I have not met many who enjoyed the journey without it having what I call a "pain anchor"—something that reminds them why they are doing this, the thing they are running away from, as well as the destination they are journeying towards.

Pain is also a funny thing. A lot of us spend our lives trying to escape it: denying that bad things happened to us, or trying to forget that they did. That's understandable, but it can also be counterproductive. Because when we harness our pain, understand it, and seek to use it to our advantage, it can be one of the most powerful forces there is. It can even bring joy if leveraged correctly.

Like many people, the formative pain in my life came during my childhood. One particularly tough moment in my life still helps me today. I was eight years old, out shopping with my mum in Bedford, a small town near where we lived. I think I had done something to annoy her but cannot remember what. One minute she was telling me that I was going to have to get home by myself, and the next she was gone. When you are left on your own as a child at that age, suddenly everyone and everything seem very big (even in Bedford). The cars seem very fast. The world becomes a very scary place when the hand you are used to holding is suddenly taken away.

I was fine that day. I found my way to the bus stop, where someone took pity on me and gave me the money for my fare. I made it home to our even smaller town of St. Neots.

But something had changed. That feeling of having been abandoned never went away. Even though it would take me years (and some therapy) to fully understand and articulate it, I think that was the day I realized I would have to look after myself in life. I needed to be independent. Although I can't imagine doing the same thing to my seven-year-old son (in fact, I probably overcompensate and hate leaving him alone, even at night), I am grateful for the pain I experienced back then, because it made me stronger today.

Another source of childhood pain came at school. It won't surprise you to learn that, as someone who isn't much good at reading and talks a lot about why the education system is broken, I wasn't brilliantly suited to the classroom. Added to that, I have dyslexia. Like a lot of people with this condition who are my age and older, that meant I spent much of my schooling being told that I was stupid. Teachers would call on me to read in class even though they knew I found it difficult, and my classmates would tease me as I stumbled over the words.

I had horrible days wondering if all the people who called me thick at school were right. But because of this pain, I adapted. I found ways to use the skills I had to compensate for the things I couldn't do. When we were given *Jane Eyre* to read and told to write an essay about it, I knew there wasn't a chance of me making it through the book. Instead, I interviewed every other member of the class about it, and did my essay about their different interpretations of the story. I got an A for that piece of work, and much more importantly I learned that there is more than one way to succeed. Much later, those skills would also help me with the work I do today, which boils down to talking to people and getting them to share their stories. Another example of how pain can be a powerful force in our lives, if we harness it right.

My last and most significant pain was the event that brought my childhood to an abrupt end: the death of my father and effectively being kicked out of my childhood home at age fifteen. This was the formative period of my life, and I often look back on it as the worst and best thing that ever happened to me, combined.

It was a horribly traumatic time, but weirdly at points I also felt completely liberated. I no longer had to go to school, live under my mum's rules, or do what other people told me. Because I had nothing, my mindset was that I had everything to gain. I would do whatever it took to make money and keep a roof over my head. It was hard, but also gloriously uncomplicated. I had no baggage, no preconceptions, and no limits.

Then there were times when reality kicked in and I felt complete despair. I was so young and had to work everything out for myself. I had no rulebook, no safety net, and no mentor. Everything I learned was through trial and error. This was the time in my life when I really, desperately needed help, and I just couldn't get it. I couldn't get a proper job, because I was yet to turn sixteen and had no National Insurance number. I didn't have the qualifications to become an apprentice or learn a trade. And there was no internet, no YouTube, no social media or any of the things we take for granted today that can connect us to a bottomless pool of information and advice (albeit it can be hard to separate the good advice from the bad online, and the internet comes with plenty of pitfalls).

I was winging it and it showed. My first business was

gardening, something I had never done before. I had just found a squat to live in, a cupboard of a room in a disintegrating house, and knew I had to make some money fast to keep even this meager roof over my head. I had no idea how this would happen, until I walked past this huge, beautiful house. Almost as soon as I had noticed it, I took in the complete mess of its front garden. I often think of this moment as the first time the entrepreneur muscle woke up in my brain. Several thoughts went through my head at once.

That garden needs cleaning up.

I could clean it up.

I could make money cleaning it up.

It's a big house so they can definitely pay me to clean it up.

Before my nerves got the better of me, I was knocking on the front door and a bemused-looking man was saying that he had meant to get around to that, and yes, he would pay me to do the job. We agreed a fee of $265 per month. $265! A fortune to me at the time.

I'd made a sale and was off and running. I didn't have a brochure or even a flyer; this was long before websites and I had no registered company. All I had was a massive need and a little bit of courage. There was just one small issue: I didn't have any tools for the job, or any money to buy them. I'd sold myself as a gardener without having so much as a spade to call my own.

Luckily, my first customer was happy to lend some tools to me, for his and all the other jobs I had been able to secure. Emboldened, I asked him for a 50 percent deposit and he agreed—it was an instinctive bit of business sense to understand that I needed cashflow. That was the first hurdle overcome, and for a few months I made money, roping in friends and the other folks in the squat I was in to help me do the work. After doing the first three gardens myself, I soon realized that I was not skilled at the work, nor did I enjoy it. That was the first time I landed on what has become a lasting business philosophy: do what you are good at and outsource the rest. In my case, I was good at making sales and encouraging people to come and work for me.

All seemed well. The business appeared to be prospering. Not knowing any better, I assumed we would go from strength to strength. Then something completely unexpected hap- pened. Winter arrived. I hadn't thought about the weather changing, or the fact that most things stop growing when it gets cold. Although there are things you can do to make money as a gardener during the winter months, I didn't know about them then. The grass withered, my work dried up, and the business died by accident, just as it had been born by chance.

It showed how naive I was, like most teenagers, and how much I hadn't thought about. Because I didn't know better and didn't have anyone to help me, I had to make all my own mis- takes. It was a good way to learn, but I've never forgotten how hard it was. The imprint of that pain has never left me. It pro- vides the foundation of the work I do and the business I run today. It's the reason I'm writing this book. I don't want any- one else to be so alone as I was at fifteen and sixteen, trying to run a business with no real idea what I was doing. I want every- one who needs help to have somewhere to go and someone to ask.

That is the importance of pain in our lives. We would never appreciate the summer as much without first enduring winter. We need to love the lows so we can truly appreciate the highs. And we need to understand both the good and bad experiences that have shaped us. Things that happened to me thirty, even forty years ago are still fundamental drivers for what I do today. I have taken that pain and made it into purpose. I've used it to power my dream of a world where we all feel liberated to give without taking. Where help is freely available to those who need it.

That is why I encourage you to think about the sources of pain in your life, ask yourself where they come from, and decide what you want to do as a result. There are few more important motives in life than the desire to right a wrong or alleviate someone's suffering. If you can find the thing that has caused you the most pain in your life, I believe you will be getting very close to finding the thing that gives you purpose, and that can propel your dream.

Question #3: How can I help others?

When we talk about dreams and purposes, it can sound a bit selfish. Like we only care about ourselves and must spend our whole lives looking inward. But that isn't true. It might take some introspection to discover your purpose and fuel your dream, but the substance of it will be the opposite of selfish.

Think of Delon, the Twitch streamer I met in McDonald's. He loved gaming, but his dream of becoming a famous streamer wasn't about him. It was about entertaining other people: putting a smile on their faces. Remember the artist I encountered in New York? Her dream of being a successful painter was driven by a purpose to fund cancer research and help other people who got the same diagnosis she had. Or consider Bradley, whose purpose was to take away people's pain as a massage therapist.

That is who we are as people. We are hard-wired to be tribal, looking for our place in the hierarchy and how we can contribute to its overall success and happiness. Most people you meet will have good intentions and want to help. The full articulation of their purpose comes when they can use their skills, their passions, and their experience to positively influence the lives of others, and the world we all live in.

A good example is people who want to start a clothing brand. That may be rooted in an individual's talent or their ideas, but it is ultimately about making people feel good when wearing the clothes, or promoting ethical materials, or using fashion as a platform to fund good causes. It's the same with people opening a restaurant: perhaps it starts with a love for making food, but it also becomes about introducing people to new cuisines, giving customers brilliant experiences, and perhaps a wider good such as providing training opportunities for disadvantaged young people or helping to feed those in need. The point is that there is often a very close link between the things we love to do and the difference we want to make in the world.

Don't get me wrong, many businesses don't have a mission to help others. But I think they are on borrowed time in the very transparent world we live in today, where everyone is connected, information travels fast, and scandals can emerge overnight. "Greed is good" is so 1980s. And be honest: do you want to be stuck running a company like that?

I don't think any business will do well going forward unless they abandon the mindset that puts profit over people. They won't find enough employees to work for them or customers to buy from them. That's why, if you dig deep into the back stories of every brand you love, you will find a story of a founder who wanted to help people in some way, and who developed that into a powerful purpose. If you want to get an idea, look up the mission statements of Patagonia compared to a fast fashion brand, or Apple against one of the brands it beat to dominate the smartphone market. The brands that you don't love will often lack this sense of purpose.

Helping people is a powerful motivation for many of us. If it wasn't, then we would never find people to do the most important jobs in society—working in healthcare, emergency services, and teaching. Let's be honest: these essential jobs are not done for the riches they bring, but because they are a way to find meaning through helping others.

As people we are sharers. One of our most fundamental instincts is to try to connect with others, help others connect to things that unite us and to support them.

That's why the last of these three questions is not about you but everyone and everything else. Other people. Plants and animals. The planet. This whole tapestry that we are woven into as human beings. We are all connected and though it might sound like a cliché it is true. We just need to be reminded of it sometimes.

The question is simple: **what can I do to help?** You can also approach it in more specific terms—what problem am I solving, what need am I meeting, what difference will I make to the people I engage with?

This is the third question for a reason. It doesn't sit in isolation but should follow directly from your answers to the previous two. The thing you like to do gives you a direction and your pain gives you a compulsion. You already have a thread. Working out what you can do to help—how you can be of service to other people and the wider world—is the answer that ties the knot.

Asking how you can help others is important not just for altruistic reasons. It's also fundamental to understand how your dream will take shape and find a place in the world. Whatever you want to do will require someone on the other side of the table. People to wear, promote, and buy your clothes; to eat your food; engage with your social media; attend your concerts; or procure your services as an architect, designer, or decorator.

Thinking about how you can help is a cheat code to step into the shoes of your future customer and work out what they want and need (and how you can give them a reason to engage above and beyond this).

It's also a way of sense-checking your dream and working out if it has any meaning for other people. That starts with potential buyers but also extends to everyone you will need to help you achieve your dream: partners, employees, endorsers, and investors. If you can work out how you want to help people, and how your dream will achieve that, then you will have a story to tell that can attract the support that any dream needs to thrive.

It also works in reverse, helping to filter out people who are not right to support you with your dream. If someone does not believe in the same things as you, it becomes an easy decision not to take their money or advice. It can help you say no to the wrong people in your life. Moral code alignment and purpose often go hand in hand and can be a good test of all those around you.

The root of your dream is going to be in something you enjoy doing, but to grow, it will need to become something that other people relate to and find interesting, useful, or meaningful. That's how it was for me as I built what began as stray bits of social media content into HelpBnk. I started asking people about their dreams because I found it interesting. I wanted to know what they would say and to see if I could help them. Then, as I did more of it, I started to pick up common themes: people were running into the same roadblocks and being limited by common forms of self-sabotage. I saw there was a chance to help people. To intervene in people's stories and encourage them to pursue their dream. To promote those success stories as a positive example for others. And ultimately to create a platform that can enable many more people to help each other, so that more dreams are encouraged and achieved.

I didn't start out with that idea. It emerged naturally through following my instincts, trying things out, and joining up some of my selfish interests with the needs I discovered. A thing I liked doing and really wanted to do led me to the thing I could do to help the most people. Now, tens of thousands of people are receiving some form of support through the platform we have built. Many of the people who get help then become helpers themselves, paying forward the free support they got.

This is why I encourage you to answer these three questions, in this order. They take you from inside to out, from the things you like and do well, to the difference you can make in the lives of others. They connect our pain and our purpose with our ability to leave a mark on the world. These are the things that durable dreams are made of.

Bonus question: How can I be sure?

After answering these questions, you might have a clear dream in your head. Or you might have an idea of the thing you want to do, which should in time lead you to your dream. In either case, you will probably have one more question: how can I be sure this is the right thing? How do I know that this is really my dream?

Nothing is certain in life, but you still want to give yourself the best chance of getting it right. Is there any way this can be guaranteed? The answer is yes and no. You will never know for sure until you try, but I believe that if you have answered the three questions carefully and identified your dream or intended direction, then you are unlikely to go far wrong.

Luckily, there is one way of double-checking that your instincts are good. You don't have to do anything and in fact it's better if you don't try. Just sit with the idea for a few days—weeks if you need to. Then wait and see what happens.

One of two things is likely to happen. Either the idea will slip out of your mind and you will hardly think about it unless you make an effort. Or the opposite will happen and you will find it hard *not* to think about this dream. You'll wake up with it on your mind; you'll be thinking about it during long meetings at work and on the treadmill at the gym. You'll find yourself making lists, jotting down ideas in your Notes app, and watching YouTube videos about it late at night. The idea has lodged in your mind and the only way to satisfy your craving is to start working towards it. You have an energy that needs to be released into something tangible. **At this point, the dream is no longer something that's easier said than done; it's easier done than said.**

This is the acid test for a burgeoning dream. If you give it the chance, your subconscious will tell you whether this is something you are seriously interested in, or if it was an idea that only sounded good on paper. Just bear in mind that, for this test to fully work, you need to be out of fight-or-flight mode, not overwhelmed by worries about how to pay the next bill. To help with this, it might help to suspend your reality for a bit: rather than thinking about your current financial situation, imagine you have $5 million sitting in your bank account. Assume that all your financial worries are wiped away. Get out of survival mode so that you can think clearly and give your dream space to breathe.

When we have really discovered our dream then there isn't any doubt. The positive side of our brain doesn't let us sit and wonder but pushes us on to find out more about the business we want to build or the career we want to launch. It will be harder to stop yourself from doing this thing than actually to do it. That is how you can be sure you have found your dream.

I promise that you will know when you've reached this point. It's one of the best feelings in the world—the absolute certainty that you are about to do something very exciting that could change your life. That you are going to do the thing you were born to achieve. At this point, you are raring to get started and your dream is ready to go from idea to reality. But first you have to create the freedom to make it happen.

6.

Free Yourself

When I met Caitlin, there was no question that she had a dream. She was young, ambitious, and knew exactly what she wanted to do with her life. She already had the name for her photography business: Chromatics by Caitlin.

As she told me when I asked about her dream, "I'd probably just travel and take pictures all the time. I'd just like to go everywhere and do photography for a living."

Why, I immediately asked, was she not doing this already?

"Because it's too hard to get to a place where you have enough money to just be able to go and do that. I'd have to get a job with a good salary and then I'd have to save . . ."

Caitlin's response was revealing. It was a version of what so many people say when I ask why they are not pursuing their dream right now. In fact, it's probably the single biggest barrier that stands between us and the thing we most want in life. We tell ourselves that we can't have it. That we'll have to build up to it and do it later (maybe). That the dream must wait until some magical "right time" in the future.

Put another way, Caitlin was trapped—trapped by all the myths we talked about earlier, by the idea that you need a job to succeed in life, and by her belief that her passion was a hobby and not a potentially profitable business. Instead of thinking about how she could achieve her dream and make it pay for itself, she was worrying about how she could afford it.

She believed photography was something that would cost her money rather than seeing that it could actually make money.

It wasn't Caitlin's fault that she thought like this. No one had ever taught her about business. Like everyone else, she had picked up the same old mantras about a steady job and hard work from school. It meant that she was disregarding some obvious ways to fund her dream and get started straight away.

The most relevant to her was sponsorship. This is a critical source of funding for many young people who want to build modern digital businesses. You might be selling photographs online, promoting a podcast, or seeking to become an influencer. What links them all is that you are creating something potentially valuable: an audience and a community that engage with you. If you do this well, brands will pay to associate themselves with you and tap into that audience. This is one of the most straightforward ways of doing what you love and getting paid to do it. Even if you don't have a following, you can do this through purpose. Find a brand that shares your purpose and ask them to support and back you now, before you are big. You will be surprised how many companies are prepared to back someone early if they can see the promise.

Sponsorship was ideal for Caitlin's dream and in our first conversation I suggested she try to get a deal with a company called lastminute.com, the first travel brand that came into my head. This was not planned or rehearsed: the name just came to me while we were talking live on camera. After we posted her video and it was seen by over 10 million on TikTok and Instagram, lastminute got in touch with her. They wanted to support her dream! And just like that, Chromatics by Caitlin was up and running. Soon she was being funded to go on photography trips to Amsterdam and Malta. She was living the dream that weeks before she hadn't believed was possible.

You might think, "She only got that sponsorship because of your following, Simon. If you hadn't promoted her, she wouldn't have stood a chance." Well, yes and no. That probably was the reason, but it doesn't mean Caitlin couldn't have found that kind of support anyway. If she had believed in her dream and asked enough of the right people to help her, eventually someone would have said yes. I had just shown her the way and speeded up the process.

The thing blocking Caitlin wasn't her lack of contacts or online following, but **her own belief that her dream was unrealistic**. This is the position so many people are in: their dream is close but they don't realize it. They are trapped in a prison of society's norms and their own doubts. They assume the thing they want to do is impossibly difficult, and they give up on it before they have even tried.

That's why, once you have done the work to define your dream, the next step is to focus on making the space to start achieving it. You need to free yourself of all the baggage that can stand between you and your dream. Not just climbing past the step you are trapped on, but doing some practical things that get you ready to chase the dream. As we will cover in this chapter, the freedom you need comes in several forms: you need to gain financial freedom, to free your mind from unhelpful preconceptions and self-sabotaging thoughts, and finally to free your idea so that people will know about it and can start to help you with it.

1. Free your finances

When people tell me that their dream is out of reach, the first reason they point to is always money. They think they can't quit their job because it represents their security in life. They think it costs a lot of money to start a business. And they think it will be a long time before they earn anything from working on their dream.

All of these beliefs are false, or at least nowhere near as true as many people claim. Take your job. That isn't safe. If the economy goes down the tubes, your employer loses a couple of major customers or needs to satisfy its investors by cutting costs, then your job will cease to exist and the company will lay you off without a second thought. Businesses have increasingly learned to talk a good game about how they treat their staff, but the basic equation never changes. To the vast majority of employers, you are only useful for as long as you help them to generate profit. If they can outsource your job or replace you with technology, they will. If you want to understand the future of your job, look at Amazon, which at the time of writing has installed a total of 750,000 robots in its factories to process packages.[1]

What about the costs of starting your own business? With so many online tools and platforms available either cheaply or for free, they have never been lower. With no technical expertise, you can build your own website and get it up and running for next to nothing. You can use freelancer marketplaces to find someone who will build you a brand at a competitive rate. And you can start building an audience and marketing yourself through social media for free.

We'll talk in more detail about the specifics of launching your business later, but the important thing to know at this point is that it can be done without very much money (and, as I have already argued, it can even be beneficial if you don't have lots of money to spend—or waste—at this early stage).

Your job, then, isn't as safe as you may believe, nor is becoming your own boss as expensive. But many people will still argue that quitting their career to start again isn't an option. This is the point I want to focus on here, because it is the crucial stumbling block for so many people who have a dream and never pursue it. They are trapped in a job that they *think* they cannot afford to quit.

Let me tell you how I've seen this play out for people. You go to university and get the good degree that you were told was essential for your career. You work hard to obtain the job in a well-paying industry—finance, consultancy, law, accountancy—that is meant to set you up for life. You do well in your career, meet a brilliant partner, and have a beautiful family, buy a great house with a massive mortgage, and go on two vacations a year. Outwardly, life seems great and that is what you will tell most people who ask. You are tired, of course, and busy, a workhorse for your employer and a chauffeur for your kids, but this is the life you dreamed of. Or so you say. The truth is that, inwardly, you are screaming. You're bored with your job, maybe even hate it outright. You're exhausted and lacking in purpose. You've got a dream but have started to give up hope that you will ever get around to it. You would quit if you could, but you can't. What about the mortgage, the vacations, the school trips?

To put it bluntly, if you carry on like this you'll never escape. Your career will become an escalator in which your salary must go up every year to keep pace with your expanding costs. You'll be terrified to get off, because who in their right mind jumps off an escalator?

Lots of people choose to stay on because it feels like the only option. They don't know that there's a version of life where you don't have to feel tired all the time, or how amazing it feels when your work is purposeful. But I know you have a dream, because you agreed not to read this book if you were 100 percent happy and fulfilled in your life. So if you *do* want to get off the escalator without falling all the way down, then let me show you how. This is how you escape the trap and free your finances: the first step to making space for your dream to flourish.

It begins with understanding one basic idea. **You need to stop selling time and start buying it.** Most people sell time: they agree to work harder and take on more responsibility for a better salary, or they stack up two or three jobs to make ends meet. They let someone else determine how much they deserve to be paid. When they need to make more money, they simply sell more time, forking over increasing amounts of their labor and energy to their employer.

The problem with selling time is that you reach a limit. You give and you give until there is nothing left. Most of the value you create gets swallowed by your employer, and most of the money they give you goes into paying the mortgage, paying for your kids, or paying into a pension that you won't see the benefit of for decades. And in the end, because you are having to give more and more to keep up, you either become unhappy with your life or burn out completely.

By contrast, people who *buy* time sell the outcome rather than the hours. They build an operation and a team that allow them to profit more without stretching themselves thinner and thinner. The people they hire, the systems they invest in, and the relationships they build allow them to buy time. They become more free as their career goes on, while those who are selling time become more trapped.

Then comes the clever bit: the most important distinction between an employee and an entrepreneur. When you work for someone else, more is expected of you the more senior you become and the more you get paid. You have to keep justifying the title and salary you worked so hard to earn in the first place. Then your salary becomes an easy target when the time comes to make cutbacks. As an entrepreneur, things can go in the opposite direction. Often, the more the business grows, the *less* is expected of you. You've built a brilliant team that's capable of running the ship without you and often does. You still own as many shares as you did before and make as much money (in fact more, because the business is growing). But you are doing less to earn it and living off all the risks you took to build the business in the first place.

That's exactly what happened to me at Fluid. After over a decade of running the business, I stepped back into the role of chairman so that we could bring in someone with a corporate background as CEO with a mandate to sell the business. I earned more in this period than at any other time in my life, while doing by far the least amount of work. All the investments I had made into my business had given me the gift of buying time. This is the career equivalent of how the superrich buy time by hiring private jets for their travel.

That's the end goal—buying time—but how do you get there?

It begins with finding a way to become your own boss. If you're not yet ready to quit employment tomorrow, then think about asking your boss for equity. And if they won't give it to you, then consider looking for a job where you can be a shareholder. Or start a side hustle where you can try out working for yourself and see what it is like to buy time.

This is something I get in trouble for saying: I have often received hate mail from business owners who don't like me telling their employees to quit their jobs or ask for equity. But I will keep on saying it, because it is one of the most important truths about life: **you should own a piece of the value you are building.** Employers know this and they rely on most of their employees either not knowing it or accepting the idea that it's not feasible (this is also what fuels the self-serving narrative of how hard it is to be your own boss). Ownership conveys freedom, and I will never apologize for encouraging more people to seek it out.

However you do it, the important thing is that you *stop selling time*. This is a system almost designed to lock you into a certain way of working that will never stop until you retire. It's a dream killer unless you choose to do something about it.

As well as learning to buy time, the second way to free your finances is a simple yet difficult one. **You have to cut costs.** All those beautiful possessions you have worked so hard to buy are traps of their own, especially if the house is mortgaged and the car is financed. Just do the numbers: say your car costs $600 per month. How many extra hours a month will that take to pay off? Frame your costs in this way and you soon realize that you are working for the bank, the car company, and anyone else you may be in debt to. It's the best incentive there is to get rid of as many of those costs and debts as possible.

This is a very difficult process for most people (me included in the past), but you are not going to achieve your dream if you have massive financial obligations hanging over your head. If the dream really matters to you, then you need to banish the most costly things from your life and accept the reality that you can live with less. This is a good litmus test for how important the dream is to you. Are you willing to do what it takes to become financially free and make space for it? When the dream is real and the purpose is strong enough, the answer to that question is going to be yes.

2. Free your mind

"How can I help you?"

The man behind the bar, good-looking and tattooed, was

asking me what I wanted to drink. Normally I am the one who asks the questions, so I couldn't help myself. I asked him about his dream. He answered without blinking: his dream was to launch his own clothing line. Then I asked him how much he needed to get started. I had cash on me that day, and the number he said matched the amount I had in my pocket. When we made a video about him and promoted his dream, it took off. I thought a story with such a lucky beginning would surely have a happy ending.

Then a few months later, he contacted me. He had spent all of the money and needed more. I realized that he had made the mistake that is so common with people at the beginning of their business journey. He had tried to act like a big company when he was building a small one.

When I ask people whose dream is a clothing business how they are going to do it, often they tell me that they need to take their design to China, get a big order processed, pay someone to brand it up, find influencers to promote it, start talking to retail buyers, and so on. At this point, they haven't even started: the business is still just an idea.

What almost none of them say is: "I've got a sewing machine; I'm going to make a few of my designs, sell them, make a few more, sell them, and just keep going."

One of those ways sounds professional, the other sounds amateur, but it's actually the second of the two that is the template for success. Look at Gymshark, one of the most successful fashion brands to have come out of the UK in recent years. Its founder, Ben Francis, got started when he was nineteen and working for Pizza Hut as a delivery driver. He bought a sewing machine and screen printer and started making the clothes in his parents' garage. He even got his grandma to teach him how to sew. Eight years later, when he sold a stake in the business, Gymshark was valued at comfortably north of $13 billion.

The moral of that story is that business can be simpler than you think. But people love to make it complicated, especially those who haven't done it before. They tell you about all the things that will be needed before they can launch a brand and make a sale. They think it costs more than it does, and it's going to be harder than it is. People tell me all the time that they need investors and hundreds of thousands of dollars to start their business. For many, this is the biggest reason not to get started in the first place.

Most of this is nonsense. And most companies are as hard as you want to make them. You can start a business right now and you can be selling to customers within days if you want to. You can experiment, learn, and improve along the way. You won't be making the clothes you sell on your kitchen table forever, but it's much better to start like that than to spend lots of time and money acting like you're Nike before you've even sold a T-shirt.

All this speaks to the crucial importance of *mindset*, which as I have said is one of the defining features of successful people. The job of starting that clothing brand from scratch is the same for everyone, but two different people may perceive it in very different ways—one as complicated, the other as straightforward; one as something that needs to be carefully planned, the other as something to get stuck into straightaway. That is why mindset matters and makes the difference.

Mindset is something you have to get right before you can hope to pursue your dream seriously. Without the right mindset, every hurdle on the journey is going to seem twice as high as it really is, and every opportunity twice as distant.

Luckily, mindset is something that you can learn. You can

train your mind so that it is ready for the challenges of pursuing a dream. After freeing your finances, freeing yourself from the trap of a poor mindset is the essential next step.

When I talk about training your mind, you probably expect that I am going to go on about pumping yourself up, having big ambitions, and being courageous. That it's all about risk, energy, and going big or going home.

So let me disappoint you. It's a bit more complicated than that. Of course you need the dream and ambition—the restless bit of your brain that is urging you on. And as I will talk about later, risk-taking is a massive part of the journey. But you also need to balance these things with more pragmatic instincts that allow you to survive to the next day and the next sale. You need to recognize that it's OK to move gradually and that a long journey can be achieved over a long time, step by step. Where other people talk about having three-, five-, or ten-year plans, you should have a whole series of one-day plans, focused on the next tangible action you can take. The next step. Do you see why I bought the staircase now?

You need that steadiness to go along with your big ambition because a massive dream simply can't be achieved in one go. It's like trying to digest a birthday cake in a single sitting. If you try, you will fail and most likely never want birthday cake again. And if you think too hard about it, you will be discouraged from even trying in the first place.

Food is a good analogy for this. If you decide to go on a diet tomorrow, then a little goal is going to be more useful than a big one. Don't say that you are going to go without potato chips, chocolate, or soft drinks for a year. Start with a day. And then another one. Build a habit and before long you will (mostly) have cut out the worst bits of your diet. Whereas if you'd started with denying yourself for the whole year, I can almost guarantee that you would slip up at some point, and then everything would become about the day you failed, not all the days you succeeded.

Again, it comes down to mindset. Whether you choose to build yourself up or tear yourself down, to make things hard on yourself or to make them achievable—it's all your choice. I personally have an addictive personality so I work to leverage that weakness. I don't drink and have never taken drugs but I do allow myself one addiction. One that I think is fun and healthy—it's called being an entrepreneur. All of us can lean into our weaknesses and even use them to our advantage. Do you bemoan yourself for being a certain way, or do you ask yourself: how can I benefit from this?

As well as being accepting of yourself, you need to be honest about how much you have to learn. Your dream may involve something you are already very good at, or something you have never tried before. Regardless, I can guarantee that you will make a lot of mistakes along the way and do things that you will later look back on with embarrassment. That's fine if you allow it to be. But so many of us don't. Again, it's a mindset issue.

This is the funny thing about having a positive disposition towards failure, growth, and learning. We understand it because we apply it to our relationships with the people we care about. If you have children, then you know that you don't laugh at your three-year-old for not being able to kick the ball properly or read a new word for the first time. You help them, encourage them, and cheer them on when they succeed. Or with a friend your own age, you probably *do* laugh when they stumble, but then you try to help them out. Like the time recently when I was getting into cycling and went out for the first time with my shoes locked onto the pedals, like a wannabe professional. I was

with a friend who is a much more experienced cyclist, and pre-
dictably, when the first hill arrived, I fell flat on my face. Once
my friend had stopped laughing (which took a while), he told
me what I needed to hear: "Next time get into a low gear before
you go up a hill." And that was the last time I fell off my bike.

We have this positive attitude with other people, recogniz-
ing that it takes help and support to succeed, but rarely do we
extend ourselves the same latitude. With our own failures, we
tend to be harsh and critical rather than supportive and understanding. We expect that we should get it right first time and
kick ourselves when we don't. Reversing that—giving yourself
the room to fail and the space to learn—is an essential step to
training your mind so it is fit to tackle a dream.

This matters because your mindset will condition how you
deal with the inevitable ups and downs on the way to achieving your dream. Will you give in to the blame game, beating
yourself up for every setback? Or will you be philosophical,
accepting that it is hard, that things will sometimes go wrong,
and that you have a lot to learn? I can promise that if you
choose the first path, you will end up burning out and giving
up long before you get close to the finish line.

Being kind to yourself, and willing to mix patience in with
your ambition, is one part of the mindset you will need. Another is having a bias towards action. Towards doing things
rather than talking about them. I always know someone is
really serious about a dream by the words they use to describe
it. They don't say "I will" or "I want to" or "I'm planning to."
They say I *am* building a fashion brand, *am* opening a bakery,
am promoting my Twitch channel, *am* training to be a pilot,
am helping to solve the homelessness crisis. They bring the future into the present, and by doing so they overcome so many
of the barriers that people put in the way of their dream. If

you make your dream something of the future, then there is a good chance it will always stay there. To avoid that, stop thinking "I will" and start saying "I am."

Ultimately, mindset is nothing more or less than the way you see the world. I believe the mindset you need to achieve a dream is one that blends optimism with realism, combines resolve with an acceptance that you will get things wrong, and that relentlessly prioritizes taking action—preferably right now. Done right, this is incredibly powerful and it's also entirely available to you. You can train your mindset and free yourself from the negative baggage that so many people carry around. You can free your mind, for free, and by doing so you will accomplish one of the most important steps towards achieving your dream.

3. Free your idea

When I go out with my microphone, I am encouraging— sometimes persuading—people to take the final step that is needed to get started with a dream: to get it out of their head and into the world. It's amazing how many people are walking around with a big idea that they are keeping secret. One morning on a commuter train, I got talking to a chef who dreamed of having his own catering company. But he was scared to try because he'd just taken on a big mortgage and his boss was telling him what a huge risk it would be to quit. When we sat and talked for a while, it soon became clear that he had everything he needed to do it. He knew this industry inside out, from ingredient costs to profit margins. He had all the knowledge and experience. He had credibility and contacts. He just needed to take one decisive step.

If you've freed your finances and trained your mind for the

task ahead, then you are almost there. But one thing remains and that is to free the idea itself: to turn the dream from something you *think about* into something you *talk about* and finally a plan you can *do something about*.

In theory this should be the simplest step, but it can also be the most difficult. People naturally fear how others will respond when they say their dream out loud. They worry about being ridiculed or not taken seriously. They think that if they expose their embryonic idea to public view and criticism, it might be destroyed on the spot.

These are understandable fears, but they are not ultimately rational. You are always going to encounter criticism, but it is only as important as you allow it to be. And the significance of it is far outweighed by what other people can do to help you with your dream once you put it in public view. **The benefits of sharing your idea and asking for help will always be greater than the costs.**

This is why I spend so much time going around encouraging people to give voice to their dreams and promoting them to our community of millions. An idea is worth nothing until you start talking to people about it and getting help from everyone who could support you along the way.

Think of Caitlin, who after saying her dream out loud was able to secure sponsorship to travel the world and take photographs. Or of Sam in Hong Kong, who within days of telling me her dream, was pitching it to a roomful of potential investors and customers. Or of the young girl who told me that her dream was to be an F1 driver: after I published her video, she got a supportive post from her hero, Lewis Hamilton. You don't need a big platform to do this. Start telling your friends, your family, and the people you work with. Vocalize the idea and state your intent.

I bet you will be surprised by the response you get. Of course there are bad actors in the world and people—especially online—who have nothing better to do than criticize other people's dreams. But the vast majority of people are good and will try to help you if they can. Never underestimate the power of those close to you to help you get a business up and running. If you tell enough people what you are planning to do, soon you will find out that your sister's friend knows a great designer, your cousin will introduce you to someone who knows about distribution, and your old schoolfriend's brother is a corporate buyer for exactly the kind of products you are planning to make. Maybe your grandma can even teach you how to sew.

That's how it was for Ronald, aka Erre Flow. When I met him, he told me about his dream to work as a DJ, but said he didn't even know how much to charge for doing a set. So I invited him to my house, had him perform for Dodge Woodall, founder of the Bournemouth 7s festival, and a week later he'd been hired to perform there. One conversation had landed him first an audition and then a gig at one of the country's major festivals. You can get that kind of help, but only if you go looking for it and are willing to share your dream. Contrary to what many people think, **it's not about who you know, it's about who you ask for help**.

There is help everywhere, and the reason I can say that with confidence is what happened after we set up HelpBnk. I'd assumed that we would have far more people signing up in search of help rather than to give help. If we were going to have a problem, it would be that we didn't have enough mentors to match demand from people who needed support. Then we opened registrations and got flooded with people who wanted to be helpers. It was the complete opposite of what we had expected and planned for. And it was a beautiful example of how help really is out there, and that people's desire to support others is incredibly strong when given the chance.

The equation is simple: if you want people to help you then you have to give them the chance. You need to state your intent, talk about your dream, and mention the challenges you expect. And you must be open to feedback and criticism, so that people with the right experience can point out where you may be going wrong or highlight something you haven't yet considered.

Some people think that they need to work in secret, doing everything for themselves and not unveiling the end result until it's perfect. They want everything to be neat and tidy, all the wrinkles ironed out, before they unleash it on the world. That's understandable if you're a sculptor or painter, but for the vast majority of businesses it's completely the wrong idea. The time you *need* help is when you are building and trying to work things out. When your "sculpture" is just a solid block with a few odd bits carved off it. When it feels like a mess. That's when you want all the help, feedback, expert advice, and support you can get.

It is hard to ask for help, and one tip I'll give you is that if you do want help from someone, don't ask them to be your mentor. That's asking them to commit more time and energy than they probably have available. Instead, ask one simple question and you will significantly improve your chances of getting a positive response. In any interaction like this, aim to leave with one key insight you didn't have before.

You have to be brave, to put your idea out there when it still feels new and vulnerable, ask for help, and expose yourself as a work-in-progress who is still learning about a lot of things. That's how everyone starts on the journey towards their dream. The ones that succeed weren't embarrassed about admitting what they didn't know and asking for help. Whereas the ones who gave up probably tried to do too much for themselves.

Even after over thirty-five years of running businesses, there are so many things I still don't know how to do. I'm happy to admit I don't know everything, because it shows I have always asked for help and found people who would support me with a particular skill or bit of knowledge. You can't be an expert in everything and you shouldn't aspire to be. Much better is to be the keeper of the dream who is capable of finding the right help and support when it is needed most. You will regret it later in life if you have a dream but don't achieve it because you never asked for assistance.

Admitting what you don't know and when you need help is just one part of opening yourself and your dream up to the world. If you are going to make any serious progress with this, then you need the kind of freedom I have discussed in this chapter: freedom in your finances, freedom in your mindset, and the freedom to share your dream even with people who may disagree with or criticize you.

Without that freedom, you are going to struggle because achieving an ambitious dream is no easy thing. And it is twice as hard if you are carrying around the baggage of heavy financial obligations or a negative attitude towards the task at hand or your own abilities. Shedding that baggage is essential. It clears the road ahead of the obstacles that are of your own making. It sets you up to tackle the actual work of getting your dream started. This is the next step we will cover: how to think about quitting your job, starting your business, and turning the dream from an idea in your head to a reality that will change your life for good.

7.

Build a Boat

Not long ago, I decided to conduct an experiment. If I offered people $2,500 on the spot to quit their job and chase their dream, how many would accept? I went to Carnaby Street in London, where I knew there was guaranteed foot traffic, and waited to see how long it would take to give the money away.

We were there all day and spoke to easily fifty people in depth. Some thought it was a joke or a scam. Others considered it seriously but decided that either it wasn't quite enough money, or they weren't confident enough to walk away, or they didn't think they could make a success of their dream. Of all those people, just one decided to take me up on the offer.

That day sticks in my mind, because it underlined how difficult the step between *having* a dream and *pursuing* that dream is for many people. Right at the moment the dream is within reach, they shrink away from it rather than running towards it. Suddenly all their worst fears about what it will be like are magnified. The possibility of failure becomes too real and they allow their doubts to drown out their ambitions. What starts as a crack in the road towards your dream soon becomes a chasm too wide to cross.

Overcoming this obstacle is the final step you must take before you can begin realizing your dream. By this point, we've covered the importance of a dream, how to draw that idea and purpose out of your life experiences, and how to create the space in your life, your finances, and your mindset for it to take root. Now it is time for action. To change your life by living your dream. To take that dangerous, thrilling, and necessary step between thinking about something and actually doing it.

It's at this point that you may encounter the idea of "burning the boats." Like the invading armies of centuries past, who sometimes set fire to their own vessels as a symbol that they refused to turn back, would-be entrepreneurs are encouraged to commit everything to their new venture and give themselves no opportunity to retreat. I agree with the substance of that, and will talk later in this chapter about the importance of going "all in" and how to achieve it.

But first I want to present you with a slightly different idea: not burning a boat but building one. Getting ready so that you will be seaworthy when you set out in search of your dream. Developing the skills, knowledge, experience, and contacts you will need to get started on your journey—the equipment that will enable you to set out without having to turn back. But nothing *more* than you need. Because this is a trip where you will need to travel light and move quickly. What I describe here is not the leisurely work of years but a matter of weeks or months to pack your bags and get ready. This is something you have to do fast if you are going to do it at all.

Step one: Get ready to quit

A lot of people ask me if they need to quit their job to follow their dream. The simple answer is yes, but it's often a bit more complicated than that.

No two people's circumstances will be exactly the same, but many of them will have a lot in common. Let me set out a few of the typical scenarios here and how I think you should act if this describes your situation.

Some people hate their job, which makes the decision easy. You should quit as soon as possible and not look back. Do this even if you don't yet feel 100 percent ready to start a business or chase your dream. Find another job, go and work for someone you respect and can learn from, and get out of the environment that is draining your spirit. No one ever regrets walking away from a bad job, and many people wish they had done so sooner.

What if you don't hate your job and are worried about losing the security it provides? Perhaps you have your dream in mind but you don't know if you are ready to go for it. This is where I want to be honest with you, and you need to be honest with yourself. **The longer you stay in that job, with that mindset, the less likely it is that your dream is going to happen.** You are in a comfort zone and its gravitational pull will become stronger the more you allow yourself to be held in place. If you don't make a conscious effort to escape this trap, then you may as well decide to give up on your dream.

That's why I say that even if you are not going to hand in your notice tomorrow, then you should proactively get ready to do so. If you want time, that's fine, but you have to make a plan to use it well. That could mean making an intensive effort to save money and build a fighting fund to launch your business. It may involve taking the first steps towards your dream as a side hustle—make those first T-shirts and sell them, run a bookstall at an open-air market to prepare yourself for opening a bookshop, start building up your social media presence and finding customers or sponsors for whatever your online business may be. Whether you are building a pot of cash, developing expertise, or making contacts in your chosen field, this is how you build a boat that will be capable of ferrying you towards your dream.

Whatever you do, *use* that time to do something and build towards your dream. I guarantee that if you simply tell yourself that you will quit by the end of the year, or in time for summer, then you are going to keep kicking the can down the road forever. You have to be honest that you are either making serious plans to pursue your dream or giving it up altogether.

Whatever you do, don't give yourself too long to do it. A good rule of thumb is that once you have decided on your dream, you should be working on it within six months. That is enough time to make any arrangements and get ready. Much longer and your resolve is going to falter or the moment is going to pass.

The months after a dream takes hold within you are a precious time. You are excited, energized, and eager to get started. If you keep making progress towards the dream, then you will sustain those feelings, like putting logs on a fire. But if you don't do anything, then the fuel will burn out and the flames will be gone. If you don't capitalize on your own energy and sense of momentum, you may never get it back. It's a bit like Andy Dufresne says in one of my favorite films, *The Shawshank Redemption*: "I guess it comes down to a simple choice, really. Get busy living or get busy dying."

I understand that walking away from full-time employment is going to be easier for some people than others. If you're in your twenties and working in a retail or service job, then you have relatively little to lose and everything to gain. Whereas if you're older and have dependents, you probably have doubts. But if you have read this far, then I know that your dream is real and that it is gnawing away at you. I promise you that this feeling of unease is not going to go away. The dream will not stay quiet however much you listen to your fears. It is human nature to worry about the consequences of a decision we are about to make, but we must also remember that regret can come from decisions that we *don't* make. We can mess up by failing to act as well as by taking action.

At this point, when you probably know exactly what your dream is and how important it is to you, inaction becomes your enemy. Getting things wrong is fine: you will learn from your mistakes, recover, and improve. But doing nothing is like digging a hole: every day it's a little deeper and harder to climb out of, no matter how much you tell yourself that you will get around to it soon. Before long, inaction becomes a habit. All you know how to do is hesitate and doubt yourself.

That is why it's so important that you *get ready* to quit your job, even if you are not quite prepared to do so yet. Make action your default setting and start putting things in motion. Make it easier for yourself to take the next step forward than to stand still.

Here's one way of doing that—a slightly crazy idea that you might need to read twice.

Don't hide what you are doing from your boss. Tell them. Say that you have a dream and that at some point you are going to quit your job to pursue it. The worst that can happen is that you will talk yourself out of a job that you were planning to leave anyway. Far more likely, in my experience, is that your boss will be encouraging and even try to support you. If you're launching a business in a similar field, your old employer could even become your first client. But either way, by doing this you have taken the kind of decisive step that is needed to start making the dream a reality.

If you still have doubts, then remember this. You got one job, and you can get another one. If for some reason the dream goes sour, or you decide that working for yourself isn't for you, then you will always be able to go back into the employment market. Let me say that again just to be clear: if you ever need a job in the future, you *will* get it. Don't let your employer or a recruiter scare you with stories about how difficult it will be. You earned a living before by using your skills and experience and you can do it again if necessary. Don't fall into the mindset that this job is so important and special that you might never do better and that it's a massive risk to leave it behind. That is the sunk cost fallacy that so many people get duped into believing: they assume that because they have put so much time and effort into getting this far that they cannot walk away now. Employers love this idea because it means good people get stuck in jobs and careers that they have outgrown. It's a belief you need to discard if you are to give your dream a chance.

Step two: Find your first customer

I still remember the very first time I asked a stranger what their dream was, not online but in the real world. In the early stages of experimenting with what I wanted to do after selling Fluid, I was spending a lot of time on different social media platforms. TikTok had recently introduced a facility that allowed people to send you tips when you went live, which I was doing to chat to people and give advice about business. At the end of one session, without realizing or wanting it, I had been sent $195.

Free money should feel good, but my immediate instinct was that I wanted to get rid of it. Even at this point, long before HelpBnk became an idea let alone a business, I knew that I wanted to do whatever I was doing for free. It was always about giving without taking: helping people with no expectation of anything in return. Although I hadn't asked for the money, I felt bad that I'd "taken" it. And I would only feel better when I made sure it went towards something good.

That thought was on my mind when I went to Tesco (a UK grocery store) to pick up a sandwich for lunch. As I scanned the shelves, I found myself standing next to a member of staff. I don't know what compelled me in that moment to approach this person, but almost on autopilot I caught her eye. It was some combination of having all these ideas floating in my head about wanting to help people, the importance of dreams, and needing to do it for free. On the way to the store, I'd withdrawn the money from a cash machine with the idea of giving it away somehow. And then I asked her the question. *What's your dream?*

It was not the typical customer inquiry and initially she seemed a bit shocked. She looked over my shoulder, as if expecting to see someone filming for a prank. But there was no camera or microphone. I hadn't planned any of this. I just blurted it out without having any idea of how she would respond or if I would ever do this again.

That was the first time I saw the power of this question. Because once the woman had reassured herself that there was nothing untoward, just this slightly weird guy asking her this unexpected question, she changed. She stood a little taller and looked me in the eye. Yes, she had a dream. She wanted to open a care home. She knew exactly the kind of culture she wanted at the home, where she wanted it to be, and what it would be called. And it all stemmed from her mother dying alone in her house: she didn't want anyone else to have that happen to them.

I was blown away. This was someone I could easily have walked by—we often do that, just passing people without a second look. Someone stacking shelves, cleaning the street, emptying garbage cans: people we wrongly assume aren't ambitious or interesting because they are doing boring jobs.

But that day I did stop and chat. I would never have guessed that the simple act of asking someone about their dream and giving them the chance to talk about it could have such a dramatic effect. I don't know if that lady has achieved her dream and has opened the care home yet. There is no record of our meeting, nor was there any further contact. Perhaps she will hear about this and let me know.

But what I do know is that the short conversation with her changed my life and helped to set the course of everything I have done since. Her instinctively open response to the question persuaded me that I should keep asking it, and that I should start filming the conversations to share the message that it's good to talk about your dreams—leveraging social media for social good.

But what, you may be asking, about the $195? When she told me about her dream, I had no doubt what I should do with it. I said that it sounded amazing, that if she opened the care home I wanted to be a customer (eventually), and that I wanted her to accept the money as a deposit.

Her single-word response was one I have heard in hundreds of similar conversations since, when I meet people and say that I want to be their first customer—that I want to pay them to take my photograph, cut my hair, paint my car, or sell me a pair of high-waisted jeans. I give them the money there and then and tell them that if they can't do whatever the job is now, we'll arrange to do it later. Almost always, the reply is the same word as the woman in Tesco used.

146

"Really?"

They cannot quite believe that someone is taking them seriously and that a real person is willing to pay them real money in return for the service they want to offer. This is perhaps the most transformative experience for anyone with a dream. The moment someone buys in to you and pays to be your first customer, your idea becomes real. You are not just aspiring to do something but actually doing it. You have arrived. And when you have done it once, you will gain the confidence to do it over and over again.

I have learned that one of the most important things I can do to help people is to become their first customer. The amounts of money that change hands are usually small and far outweighed by the transfer of trust and belief. A person with a dream has an idea. One with a customer has the beginnings of a business that can make that dream a reality. It's just a single step, but often one of the most important and meaningful.

That's why I believe an important part of building your boat is to find that first customer, wherever they may be and however you find them. It could be a friend of a friend, someone you connect with on social media, a current or former colleague. You can even make your mum or dad your customer—just don't give them a discount.

Find that customer, get them on board, and I promise it will change how you perceive yourself and the business you want to build. You will gain confidence, because there is nothing like doing something to realize it's not as difficult or complicated as you had assumed. You will learn, because there is nothing like having customers to find out what people really want and how they want it. And you will develop an appetite to do more, because there is nothing like having one customer to make you want to find two, and then four, and so on. One caveat to this is that your dream might be charity-related and you might not think you need a customer in the conventional sense, but you do need all sorts of people—donors, trustees, volunteers. Go and seek out one of them.

This is something you can do whether you are quitting your job tomorrow or don't plan to do so for another six months. Secure your first customer and make your first sale. When you do, suddenly the dream goes from being something that existed in theory to something that is happening in reality. You are achieving your dream. You have begun.

Step three: Go all in

Over my career I have built nineteen businesses in contrasting fields, different parts of the world, and varying sizes. I am still learning, but I like to think I know what I'm doing. Here is one thing I am absolutely certain about. You cannot build a company part-time. If you asked me to do it, even with all my experience, contacts, and resources, I would fail.

You might be able to start a business as a side hustle, gaining the kind of experience and confidence I have described, but you will quickly hit a ceiling. Once you are past the euphoria of that first customer and trying to build something serious, you will find that the needs of the business cannot be squeezed into the hours before and after work, on weekends and days off. You have to go all in.

Businesses are a bit like babies. They constantly require your attention and you can't take your eyes off them for too long. When you are running your own company, you will learn the true meaning of the phrase "stuff happens." Orders will fail, customers will be unhappy (rightly or wrongly), there will be a crisis with one of your suppliers, someone won't turn up where you need them to, and you won't get paid on time. Some combination of all these things will happen to you most weeks, and you have to be ready to jump on the problem and deal with it.

And those are just things that get in the way of the job you set out to do: to sell a great product or service, to make your customers deliriously happy, to build your brand, nurture your network, and take the next step towards your dream.

Now imagine doing all of that part-time. Imagine having your existing job and trying to run your business on the side. You can't, not if the business is going to get any traction and grow into something serious.

That's the practical reason why I say you need to go all in if you are going to make a success of your business and in turn your dream. You need to be ready to devote your whole attention, energy, and creativity to this project. Nothing less than 100 percent of yourself is going to be enough.

Being all in is necessary to make progress, and it's also a statement of intent to everyone you want to work with and support you. When you are hiring people and trying to attract customers and investors, the first question people will ask themselves is whether you are serious. Do you really mean what you say? Are they making the right decision if they choose to work for you, buy from you, or invest money in you? The easiest way to kill their belief stone dead is to say that you are doing it part-time. To say, in effect, that you want them to make a commitment that you are not willing to make yourself. As someone who has invested in dozens of businesses, I can promise you that one of the first things I look for is how dedicated, trustworthy, and purposeful the person behind it is. If I have any doubt at all about this, I will run a mile.

Going all in is also a commitment to yourself. It says that you have faith in the idea, you believe in the dream, and you will do everything in your power to achieve it. You may fail, or discover that the business you tried to build wasn't the ultimate vessel for your dream. That's fine because you will learn and do better the next time. What isn't fine is not giving yourself the opportunity to succeed. When you have an idea that you can't get out of your head but are too timid to pursue it. You can (and should) forgive yourself for failure, but you may never forgive yourself for not trying when you had the chance.

The final reason to go all in is accountability. At some point, you have to find out whether you can make this idea work, and if you are capable of making money out of it. All the thinking, hoping, and planning in the world won't substitute for testing yourself in the real world. You need to be in that slightly scary position where you are in trouble if the business doesn't make money. That kind of tension—where you don't just want to succeed but really need to—can't be simulated. You have to take off the stabilizers and accept the risk of toppling over.

Those are the reasons for going all in, but how do you actually do it?

The first thing, which sounds simple but is incredibly important, is that you should tell people. Say what you are doing and what you hope to achieve. Do this loudly and often. Tell your friends, family, and work colleagues. Tell your postman, the barista at your favorite coffee shop, the people you say hello to at the gym. Tell your dog.

You have to do this because it makes it real. Even the simple act of talking about your idea serves to get it out of your head and into the world. It invites feedback, including things you may not have thought about, or suggestions of people you should meet or competitors you should check out. And it makes you accountable. A few weeks or months down the line, people will ask you how it's going. You'll know they will ask and you will want to have a good answer.

After the talk should come the action. This is where I am going to get myself into trouble with a lot of people, when I say that there is something you *shouldn't* do. Don't write a business plan. Don't spend time on it. Don't convince yourself that it's important or necessary.

One thing I have learned about business is that people *love* plans. The longer they are, the more fancily decorated with charts, the more they are filled with numbers, the better. The business plan is supposed to be the font of all knowledge: a guarantee that you have thought of everything, planned for all eventualities, and given yourself the best possible chance of success.

The problem is that this is nonsense and so are most business plans. I have read hundreds and even the good ones are full of stuff you don't need to get started, or with projections that have almost no chance of becoming true. Business plans pretend that you can know what is going to happen five years from now, when most entrepreneurs will tell you that it's hard to be sure about the next five weeks. Even worse, they are a form of distraction from the actual work of starting a business. It gives the illusion of progress when in fact you are doing almost nothing. Remember what I said earlier—what you really need is a north star, a purpose. Write it on your wall and call it a business plan if you like.

Instead of writing a plan, you should *prepare* to launch your business. Do stuff! Find out how much things cost, where a good location for your shop might be if you need one, and what the current trends are in your industry. Do the best kind of research there is, where you actually go and try things and talk to people. Gather data and hone your instincts. But don't sit at your desk and write a plan. Take actions instead: meet people, check out the competition, focus on developing your product or trialing your service. Launch the business in your head, not on paper. Go out there and find out how the market works. Learn by observing and doing. If you don't have any experience in the sector, consider working in it for a little while. Although I've talked a lot about quitting your job when the time is right, it's a perfectly sensible path to take a job for a while if it will give you the experience and confidence you need to pursue the dream.

These actions may be small, but each one of them—even if it is just a conversation, a site visit, or a social media account registered—will take you towards the point when you are ready to go. They all help to develop your confidence, your intent, and your understanding of the business you are about to launch. To build the boat that will get you started. It may sound like a paradox, but going all in is not something you do suddenly. In most cases, it will be something you build up to gradually and carefully, just like you are going to make sure you are securely strapped to a parachute and a reserve before attempting a skydive.

But once that preparation is done, you need to be ready to jump. There comes a point where it is a case of go or no-go. You either do it or you don't. My hunch is that the longer it has taken you to reach this point, the more likely you are to step back rather than forward. The more you have waited and given yourself time to prepare, the more you were subconsciously doubting yourself.

If you hesitate and delay, you are also giving life the chance to catch up with you. You won't believe how things will start happening to you just at the moment when you are getting ready to launch a business and pursue your dream. There will be an illness in the family, a pipe will burst in your house, your car will break down, or one of your friends will go through a crisis and need your help. I can almost guarantee that something is going to come around that seems designed to try and stop you from chasing your dream. If you're not already 100 percent committed to the task, then you are going to falter and even give up entirely.

That is why I say you have to build a boat, do it as quickly as possible, and then get started. Commit until there is no turning back. That is the level of certainty you will need if you are going to make your dream into a reality. There can be no questions now. This is your purpose, your direction. This has to work and you are going to make it happen.

When you have that feeling—of excitement mixed with a little trepidation—then you know that you have got the balance right. The butterflies will tell you that you have prepared well enough to be confident at the same time as taking a big enough leap to be a bit scared. Too confident and you will become complacent; too fearful and you will be unable to move. Right in the middle is where you want to be. And now your vessel is seaworthy, your direction is set and you are ready to go. Your dream lies ahead.

Warning #2

If you have reached this point and you're not sure about your dream or your purpose, then you need to pause here. Everything that's contained in the final part of the book is based on the premise that you have worked these things out. If you haven't, it won't help you.

If this describes you, then don't despair. My advice is go and work for someone whose purpose you admire and respect. Find ways to help people. Unlock different "muscles" in your brain until you are ready to answer the three questions, state your purpose, and define your dream.

And if you're wavering, then here is a quick checklist for those who think they are ready to proceed—a parachute kit, if you will. Read on if:

1. Your purpose is clear and you can describe your dream.
2. You have a community of friends, family, and supporters behind you.
3. You have the validation of one customer or person who is willing to back you.
4. You have gotten your costs down, and have a few months of cash in the bank.
5. You believe in yourself.

If you meet those criteria, then pat yourself on the back and turn the page. And get ready: this is the best bit.

PART THREE

Follow That Dream

How to build a business that will fulfill your dream

8.

Start Poor

As we head into the final section of the book, let's catch up.

You have your idea.

You have your dream and the purpose that will drive it.

You've made a start and you're ready to go all in.

Now you probably have a few big questions left. Can I really do this? How do I make it real? How do I pay for it?

Whatever your dream may be, I promise that you can either make money from doing it or you can find a way to fund it. Whatever people try to tell you, your passion can be a serious business and your dream can become a proper job. There will be a business model that can support and enable your dream. This final section of the book is dedicated to helping you find that model, scale it up, and create a commercial vehicle that can drive you on towards the dream.

Some people treat "business" as a dirty word, but in the way modern society is set up, it is also the best mechanism we have for helping people and doing good. Everything I now do is based around trying to help people for free: people can go on Helpbnk.com to get advice, they can ask me questions on social media, and they can ring the doorbell to pitch their dream. I will never charge them for the help, advice, or promotion they receive. While we have a subscription tier for those who want to support us, all the knowledge I provide is always available for free.

But to *do* all of that, to build and maintain the platform, produce the content, and connect people to sources of help, is far from free. In fact, it's pretty expensive. I have to pay great people so I can have a team who turns all my bad ideas into good ones. I have to pay hosting costs that increase the bigger our community becomes. I have to buy equipment, keep the lights on at an office, keep people fed and watered, and so on.

So although what I do sounds a bit like a charity, from the beginning I have run HelpBnk and the work around it as a business. My primary business model is sponsorship: brands that believe in what I am doing and want visibility with my community pay for me to promote them. And that allows me to offer everything I do with the community for free. Rather than detracting from purpose, as a lot of people think a for-profit business model must do, I believe that making money helps me to deliver my purpose and continue doing it in bigger and better ways. The more profit I make, the more capital I can (and do) invest in helping people with their dreams.

I am not telling you this to puff myself up, but to explain why I will spend the remainder of this book showing you how to create a business model that can support and enable your dream. Because whatever your vision may be—even if it involves doing something for free—it will need a commercial anchor. Having a dream doesn't magically mean you get to stop paying for things.

The reality is that you can only fully achieve your dream if you make it the big priority of your life. You need the *freedom* to do the thing you love and not be worried about the consequences. You will earn that freedom by making money as you go, and ensuring your dream is sustainable. That's why you are almost certainly going to have to build a business to help you achieve your dream, or to develop a business model (as nonprofits and charities do). Even if you don't think of your dream as a business idea or yourself as an entrepreneur, you will need a business approach at some level. You need people to pay for your work, whether as customers, subscribers, or sponsors. You need to build a personal brand. And you need a community either of supporters or clients. I've never heard a dream that didn't require some kind of business to support it.

The good news is that this is easier and more achievable than you may think. That's because all the worst things you've heard about starting and running a business are wrong. It's not true that it costs a lot of money to launch a business. It's not true that almost all fail within the first year. And it's not true that you need some kind of special entrepreneurial gene to do it.

In fact, as I will explain, it's quicker, less expensive, and more realistic to start a business than almost anyone has told you. That doesn't mean you will be cutting corners or building on sand. In fact, working on a shoestring will *help* you build a foundation for success over the long term. It's by starting your business poor that you will give yourself the best chance of striking it rich in the end. This chapter is about how to get started, and why it's essential that you don't break the bank in doing so.

Why you need to start poor

Before we get to the "how," a word on the "why." Why am I telling you to think poor and act cheap when you start this business? A cautionary tale may help to explain. Of all the businesses I have run, there was only one that I ran with a "rich" mentality, acting as if money was no object. It wasn't long before I regretted it.

Remember *DevaShard*, the comic book that was my most expensive failure? That didn't start as my idea. It was part of a joint venture that we had entered into at Fluid with a very successful entrepreneur in Hong Kong. We got to know him as a client of our agency, and soon he was talking about doing all his marketing work with us. This was a seriously successful man, the owner of a private equity firm who had done deals running into not just the millions but hundreds of millions. He had big ideas spanning sport, entertainment, hospitality, and more. And he wanted to work with us on all of them. He didn't want to be a traditional client but a business partner.

When he proposed a joint venture as the vehicle to work on these projects together, we jumped at what felt like a big opportunity. This was a chance to take our business to the next level. Working with major global brands such as Estée Lauder was one thing, but we were never going to be more than a supplier to them. Here, we were being offered an equity stake in ambitious business ideas that could far exceed what we had created so far. There was the comic book business, which he had dreamed up and was eager to make a reality. A potential restaurant chain. A sports management agency and television rights to a new cricket tournament. We would pursue all of these as joint ventures, through a sister company to Fluid. I'll always remember what he said to me on the day we signed the paperwork to set up the new business: "Let's put this away and never look at it again."

Best of all, or so it seemed, we would not have to do this on the cheap. With our new partner's financial firepower behind us, there would be no more bootstrapping our way to success, spending only what we had earned and making the business pay for itself. This time we could invest, spending in anticipation of revenue, not limited to taking one small step at a time.

Soon we were making full use of that checkbook: we leased a fancy office with a gym and cinema room, big enough for twenty-five, though at the time we only had three people on the team. As is customary in Hong Kong, we hired a feng shui master to come and advise us on the design and layout of the office, and how to make the most creative and harmonious space possible. I honestly felt like this was the business I had been waiting my whole life to run. It was ambitious, we had money to spend, and there were no limits. This was how they operated in Silicon Valley. Wasn't it?

DevaShard was the first project we pursued through this flashy joint venture. As you know, it didn't succeed. And as the prospect of our comic book becoming a hit movie drained away, I began to hear less and less from our business partner. Before long, I'm afraid to say, we were engaged in a legal dispute. *DevaShard* turned out to be the first and last project of our once ambitious joint venture. We wound down the new company and were lucky that the landlord allowed us to break the lease on our expensive office, which had never operated at anything near full capacity.

That experience wasn't just an object lesson in picking your partners with care. It was also a warning about not running before you can walk in business and not spending money you don't have. I'd been seduced not just by a wealthy business partner and big ideas, but by the thought that I didn't have to worry anymore about justifying every cost. I lost my discipline and stopped listening to the business instincts I had built up over twenty years. I got complacent, because it felt like spending money wasn't costing me anything (though in the end it definitely did, and we ate a seven-figure loss). That failure taught me many lessons, and one of the most important was that I could never indulge in this rich person's mindset to

starting a business—one that tells you money is no object because you will make it back later.

Before the joint venture, I had bootstrapped every business
I had run (taking on no outside investment and relying on savings and the profits we generated), and since then I have gone
back to that model. It's the best way of making sure that you
are building a sustainable business that pays for itself, and that
you can scale over time on strong foundations, not having your
mistakes covered up by someone else's money. It sounds counterintuitive, but **not having money can be an advantage** in the
early stages of running a business. It means you justify every
penny you spend and won't do anything that doesn't contribute to the bottom line. Where deep pockets make you complacent, a lack of capital sharpens your mind and guarantees your
discipline. As mentioned earlier in this book, you only have to
look at start-up implosions like WeWork and Juul to see why
having lots of money doesn't guarantee success.

While there are certain companies that do require significant upfront costs, in complex hardware or research and development, that isn't going to be relevant for 99.9 percent of the
people reading this book. For almost all of you, the dream you
are pursuing and the business you are launching can and should
be bootstrapped. You should start it poor, wasting nothing and
earning everything. In this chapter, I will explain how.

How to define your business model

Before you can start bootstrapping your business, you need to
know what kind of business you intend to run—to define your
business model. Or in simple terms: how are you going to
make money while pursuing your dream? This is going to

involve selling something, but you need to define *what* you are selling, *who* the customer is, *where* those sales are going to happen, and *how* the money comes back to you. Let's look at each of these in turn.

The question of what you sell sounds simple, but there is often a nuance. You may think that you are just selling a pair of shoes, a piece of jewelry, or a recipe kit, but a product is rarely just a product. People want to know who made it and what inspired them. They want to know your story, which means you are selling yourself as well as your creation. That's equally true if you are running a service business, whether you are re-fitting bathrooms or devising marketing campaigns. People want to do business with someone they trust, and it's never just about the work but who is behind it. You need to nurture a personal brand and get used to selling yourself as much as the product or service. Why are you the one they should trust? What makes you different? What is your motivation?

This is even more true if you are trying to be a content creator and influencer of some kind, because then your business is effectively you—your personality, your style, and your ability to engage and entertain people. Every founder-run business at some level involves selling the individual as well as the product or service. That means you need to think about your personal brand and how to make your ideas, your story, and your dream visible to your customers. Remember that people buy from people.

Who is the customer and where are the sales going to happen? These are perhaps the most important questions for any fledgling business. They throw up all sorts of choices that will quickly define what kind of company you will be running, supported by what kind of revenue model.

You would be amazed by how many businesses don't think enough about who their customers are. They either guess, make assumptions, or take for granted that people will be interested in their product or service. This is a shocking oversight, because you can't sell something if you don't understand who you are selling it to. Making a sale is hard when you are trying to push something onto a random audience, but it's easy when you are talking to a customer you have hand-picked and taken the time to understand—when you can solve their problem, meet their need, or give them something that will make them happy. At that point, you don't really have to sell at all.

Knowing the customer is the cornerstone of any business, so where do you start? It's tempting to say that *everyone* should be your customer, because who doesn't want the biggest possible market? But it's rarely that simple. There's a good reason why many businesses don't want just anybody to buy their product. Ferrari doesn't want to sell cars to parents doing the school run, for example. That's because their brand is about luxury and exclusivity. For the same reason, you'll never see Volvo sponsoring a Formula 1 team: their cars are about keeping your family safe, not how fast they can go from zero to sixty.

The lesson here is that your brand, and your business, need to reflect its customers to appeal to them. Teens are not going to buy shirts from the same label as their grandparents. They are going to hang out in different coffee shops from parents with strollers. It's futile to think you can have it all and appeal to everyone. Much better to start in one niche and build a brand that appeals to a defined audience with particular needs and interests. Then you can design your products and build your marketing around these people. You can, as we will discuss later, build a community of customers with shared interests and experiences. When you think about your customer, be as specific as possible. Imagine the people you want walking into your café or browsing your online store. Where do they buy their lunch, what other brands do they like, how do they spend their weekends?

Don't worry about being stuck in this niche forever: if you are successful, over time you can expand and diversify. Gymshark started out by selling clothes for male weightlifters. Over time, it began to cater for general gym users and has since developed a successful line for women. Lululemon has gone in the other direction: having built its brand around yoga pants for women, it now also sells a whole range of active and formal wear to men.

This all assumes you are trying to sell to individual customers. That's probably how your business will start, whether by setting up a market stall or driving people to an online store. But it may not be your ultimate business model, which brings us to the question of *where* your sales will happen. Selling to individuals is hard work and over time you may graduate to more efficient approaches that allow you to reach more customers in one go—selling not direct to the consumer but through a business that is already serving large numbers of the right people: restaurants, cafés, supermarkets, major retailers. You still need to know who the consumer is and how your product appeals to them, but at this stage your actual customer is the one you are supplying—a corporate "buyer" or a small business owner, not an individual consumer. That means in turn you need to understand *their* needs and priorities, and how you can make your T-shirt/moisturizer/pasta sauce/children's toy appeal to them.

That is why I say you need to understand your business model. Until you know exactly what you are selling, to what customer, and through what channel, you are not going to be ready. And when I say *know exactly*, I mean that you can not only pitch the product to your typical customer, but know in advance what questions they are going to ask, have your answers ready, and understand what is going to reassure and convince them.

All that covers one kind of business model, where you are selling a product or service directly to a customer or through an intermediary. That is how most people think about business, but it's far from the only model. There are many other approaches that may be more suitable ways for you to build a business and fund your dream.

One we have already touched on is sponsorship. If you are building an audience and a community with lots of shared interests, then there is a good chance that brands will pay to be associated with you and for you to promote them to your community. They will pay you money to be mentioned in your videos or have their logo on your website and at your events. They want to access exactly the kind of people you are bringing together—whether that is football fans, music enthusiasts, dog lovers, or fashionistas—and they will pay for that privilege.

Closely related to this is the advertising model, one that the entire internet economy has been built on. The reason that Google can offer most of its services for free is that it earns well over $200 billion each year in advertising. It guarantees an audience, and advertisers pay to access it, which allows the company to let consumers use Google Search, Maps, Gmail, and YouTube without charging them. The advertisers are paying for it (and as a consumer, you have to pay extra to get the product without ads). What's good for the tech giants can also be good for you. If you are bringing people to your platform, then you have the chance to make money by selling advertising. It's one of the oldest business models there is.

Creators of various kinds may also want to consider a licensing model, where companies will pay them to use their designs, images, or words for their own purposes. If you have created something brilliant and people want to use it, then you can charge them for it. Licensing is one of the big ways people make money in all forms of media, from photographers to musicians, writers, and filmmakers.

Another business model is subscription. We all know how this works because of services like Netflix: pay a regular fee in return for access to something you want. If you're creating unique content in any form—whether it's a newsletter, a podcast, film, music, or art—then you may be able to build up a community, of which some members will pay to have regular or privileged access to your work. Platforms such as Patreon, Substack, and Twitch are designed to support exactly this kind of business model (although of course they take a cut of your income as part of their own model).

That is not an exhaustive list, but you get the idea. There are plenty of ways to monetize your idea and start getting paid to do what you love. And of course, there is no obligation just to pick one of them. A talented musician or photographer might choose to spend some of their time building up an online community with an eye to gaining paid subscribers, at the same time as taking paid commissions from companies who want particular images or pieces of music to be created, and working on their own content that they make available to be licensed. A food business may start selling its wares from a mobile kitchen and grow over time by distributing through retailers and opening one or several restaurants. Your business doesn't just have to be one thing, and in an ideal world you will develop multiple income streams to make your dream more resilient.

The important thing is that you start with a clear idea of what business model or models you want to pursue, who your potential paying customers are, and where you can expect to find them. Nothing is guaranteed and you will have to work out plenty of things along the way through trial and error. But if you get these essential things right at the beginning, then you at least have a compass to navigate with. And then you can start doing things—preferably as cheaply as possible.

How to get started for free (almost)

A few decades ago, you would have started a business by renting an office, having telephone lines installed, and even hiring a secretary. Today, you can set up that business from the laptop you already own, using the internet connection you are already paying for, and harnessing the online services that connect you to the whole world at the touch of a few buttons. That's what I mean by starting poor. **You don't have to spend a lot of money to make your business real.** Most of the things you need right at the beginning are either free or pretty cheap.

Being cheap, and acting poor, begins with doing everything you can that comes for free. In our digital world, that includes more things than ever. You can register social media handles and start creating and promoting content without spending anything. You can use free trials to get a website designed and launched. You can contact potential customers and partners via email. In other words, you can have what is essentially a functioning business up and running without spending anything, other than the $250 or so that it costs in the United States to register as a company (and if you are going to operate without staff to begin with, using your legal name for the business, you won't need to register at all).

Obviously, not everything is completely free. You might want to pay for an accountant to make sure you have everything

financially fine-tuned (I have done this with almost every business I have run, and never regretted it). You might choose to
spend a bit of money having a designer create a logo and spruce
up your website. You might want to experiment with putting
some of your budget into online advertising to push your content. It may also be the case that you have to purchase certain
equipment that's necessary for your work. But my point is that
you can do almost everything you need to do either for free or
for very little. Remember to think in terms of wants vs. needs.
Do I need this thing to make my business successful, or do I just
want it because it will make me feel or look good? If you don't
need it, don't spend money on it. You will thank yourself later
(and so will your accountant when you get one).

Having this bootstrapping, penny-pinching mindset isn't
just about keeping your costs down in the early stages. It's also
about taking a pragmatic, efficient approach to how you seek
out customers, strike deals, and do your work.

With one of our first customers at Fluid, I agreed to do the
work for free. A lot of people tell you not to do this: they say
that if you don't charge for the work, people will never value
it. I don't agree. Sometimes, doing something for nothing is
the gesture that can build trust and one that will pay you back
many times over. In the case of that client, they stayed with us
for sixteen years, did a huge amount of lucrative business, and
became one of our best customer references. We profited in
the long run because we had practiced delayed gratification:
by starting poor, we helped to ensure the rewards would come
later.

The same ethos should apply when it comes to all aspects of
your early business journey. Be sensible, lay deep foundations,
and don't chase trends and shortcuts. This can be harder than it
sounds, because human nature means we are easily attracted

by things that look flashy and interesting. We chase novelties and fads, assuming that success will come if only we can emulate the latest viral video format and get millions of eyeballs on our business from the word go.

The problem with such temptations is that they will often mean you take your eye off the ball. Not long ago, I was approached by someone who was setting up a business with a niche product—a moss plant—designed to make your bathroom smell better without chemicals. They wanted my advice for how to go viral with it on social media. I told them that TikTok wouldn't be my first port of call for this kind of business. They needed customers, so they should go somewhere they knew those customers would be. In their position, I would contact my local garden center. They had been in business for fifteen years and would have thousands of customers on their mailing list. Those were exactly the kind of people this business needed. So why not do a partnership with the garden center, or, better still, a dozen like it, and give them a revenue share to market and distribute the product? Why spend months or years posting on social media and trying to find customers when someone already has the database of clients you want? Focus is key in these early stages of growing a business, so don't run before you can walk or overcomplicate things.

The mindset you need is to be nimble, decisive, and willing to adapt constantly. Don't try to follow an exhaustive plan, acting like you are a big and established brand. Just get started and try things.

Exactly what you should be doing depends on the kind of business you are running. The customers you want might be hanging out in online communities or they could be walking down the street. You might be better off paying for ads on social media or handing out flyers at a train station. If in doubt, try different approaches, gather data, and do more of what works.

Don't forget that you are not the first person in the world who has washed a window, opened a coffee shop, or sold a T-shirt. And you are not the only person in your zip code trying to do it right now. Understand the market you are going into, the businesses already in it, and the customers they are serving. Are those companies your competitors or could they be partners? Could you help them with customers they don't have the capacity to service? Might they want to stock your products, or enter into some kind of revenue-sharing agreement for business you can do together? Especially with other small businesses, there is often more flexibility than you would think. If you can bring an offer to the table that gives someone else value and upside without requiring too much from them, they are going to take it seriously. Good partnerships are worth their weight in gold: often in business, $1 + 1 = 11$. Try to find those force multipliers rather than doing everything on your own.

This need to be nimble and flexible is the reason that, rather than writing an unwieldy business plan, I prefer to make a mind map when I'm working on a new company. This is nothing complicated, just a series of connected circles that begin with the thing I like doing (the "hobby"), expand out to the things I can do to make money (the business model), and then link again to the people, partners, customers, and others who can help me to make it happen. These are quick to do and if you are a visual learner they help you to understand the connections that underpin any successful business. How does your hobby become a business that makes money? How and where do you find customers? Which existing businesses in your area and industry could you partner with? Who might your sponsors or advertisers be? What kind of skills do you need to complement your own and what people might you therefore need to hire? So many of these things are linked to one another, and a mind map helps you figure out what you need and where to go next.

Alongside your mind map, write down every question you have about the business you want to run. How will you make your products? What regulations do you need to meet? What should your pricing structure be? Where and how will you sell? How much cash do you need to generate to be sustainable? Write them down and then find someone who can give you the answer. Do your research, ask people for help, and don't be afraid to admit what you don't know. Kill your ego and admit where you are ignorant.

Finally, write down some ideas for unconventional, random, and slightly crazy things. I know that when you're starting a business for the first time, it sometimes feels like you have to act a certain way, and that everything needs to be grown-up and professional. The problem with this is that you can easily forget about humor, personality, and the importance of grabbing people's attention in a busy world. Every business should have one idea that is a bit wacky and designed to promote you in a different way. Stage a protest about an issue affecting your customers. Try to break a world record in your field. Arrange a photo opportunity that social media won't be able to resist. It doesn't even have to be directly related to what you are doing: famously, Airbnb helped to fund itself by selling boxes of cereal featuring Barack Obama and John McCain, the candidates in the 2008 US presidential election.

Most importantly, whatever you are trying to do and however you want to do it, *just start*. I talk to so many people who are thinking about a business but not doing it. They tell me about all the things they need before they can get going, rather than focusing on what they can do right now. If you only take one message away from this chapter, it's that you should get going as quickly as possible and do as many things as possible to build momentum. It doesn't have to be the perfect business from day one, and it might not even be the business you ultimately end up running. You probably haven't worked everything out and you are bound to make mistakes. But you will learn so much from the experience of running a business: making sales, dealing with customers, and encountering the unexpected. **A day of doing things is worth a month of planning to do them.** And the best way to become an entrepreneur is to start being an entrepreneur.

Why three is the magic number

Let's say you have been doing all the things I've suggested in this chapter. You've done your mind map, studied your market, established contacts with potential partners, and dabbled in marketing. Hopefully you've also made your first couple of sales. Now you're probably wondering: at what point is this real? When can I say this is no longer a hobby or an experiment but an actual business?

My answer to that question is another question: how many customers do you have?

The first customer, as I suggested earlier, shows you that the business can be more than an idea in your head. The second proves it wasn't a fluke. But I think it's the third customer that really makes your business real and puts your dream on solid ground.

Three, as they say, is a crowd and there are several reasons why you need a crowd of customers to validate your business and turn your idea into something that people really want to engage with.

First and foremost, that small crowd will give you the most important information you need to make a business successful: what does your customer actually want?

As an entrepreneur, you may think that you know this. After all, you've been walking around for months if not years with this idea in your head. You think that you can bring something to the market that it has been missing: a piece of software that solves an annoying problem, a new food concept people won't be able to resist, a fashion label that is bound to go viral. You've told your friends and family and they have said it sounds like a great idea. They'd buy it. You're confident: you've seen an opportunity and you're going to be the one to grab it.

What you haven't done is sold that product, concept, or experience to a real customer who has no allegiance to you. You haven't found out if they would buy it again or recommend it to a friend. You haven't seen it through the eyes of the customer, the individual (or organization) who will determine the fate of your business. You have your dream, but you haven't sold anyone on it yet.

This is the test that every new business must pass. There comes a point when you have to see if the world actually likes your idea. Do people agree that the problem you have identified is a problem, or that the solution you are offering will work? Do they get excited about the things you believe are new and interesting? Will they share your view that there really is a simpler way to pay their bills, book their trip, or get their car repaired? Do they buy into your dream enough to part with their money?

Until you ask (in this case by starting to sell to real-life customers), you will never know. And once you start, you might be surprised about what you hear. That is the funny thing about customers. They don't always behave the way you expect or want. They don't necessarily ask for the things you anticipated.

All this means that the idea you start with and the product or service you end up with may be some distance apart. Ultimately, it's the customer that will lead you to where you want to be, showing you how their actual needs and preferences intersect with the thing you were planning to build. **You have to know who your customer is rather than who you expected them to be.**

How can you be sure that what one customer wants will match what the next one needs? Well, you can't, and one of the lessons of building a business is that you cannot please everyone and the customer is *not* always right. If you keep adding a tweak here and a modification there, soon you will end up with the car that Homer Simpson designed.

The challenge for any entrepreneur is to be responsive to customer feedback while avoiding the fate of trying (and failing) to be all things to all people. And that is why I think you need three customers. One might be an anomaly, and the second may not tell you anything interesting. But once you are serving three customers, you will have a reasonable idea of your market, its needs and preferences. You will have the minimum level of feedback you need to understand if your idea will work, what you may need to adjust, and how your business can succeed. If you can make those customers happy, then there is every chance that you will soon have added another three, and then another. Now your business is really off and running. And the next question on your mind is: how do I make it grow?

9.

Grow Rich

I still remember the very first video that I posted to YouTube, when I was starting out with content creation and all the work that would become HelpBnk. I spent days on it, trying to get the edit just right, tweaking little details like the title and thumbnail picture that experts will tell you are the key to success. I thought that all this painstaking effort was bound to be rewarded.

Do you want to know how many views I earned for this hard work? It certainly wasn't millions, in fact it wasn't even thousands. I had hoped, and maybe even expected, to reach a big audience. But after a week, my video had been viewed by a grand total of just 150 people. My pride and joy was just another piece of chaff floating through the wasteland of social media. It had been a complete waste of time.

Or had it? Just as I was bemoaning my inability to get any eyeballs on the video, a DM dropped from a stranger. They'd watched it. It had inspired them. Now they were going to have a serious go at the business idea they'd been toying with. One person. It didn't seem like much. But at the time it felt like everything. I was over the moon. Perhaps all that effort hadn't been wasted after all.

I say this because people often have the wrong idea about what it takes to grow a business. They make the measures of success bigger and more complicated than they need to be.

They intimidate themselves by setting unrealistic targets like hitting a million dollars in turnover within twelve months, getting thousands of subscribers or growing revenue at hundreds of percent year-on-year. There is a macho element to business that makes people believe they must be failing if they're not hitting some hugely ambitious yardstick. There are too many people out there selling the idea that success is hard and the only kind of growth that matters is turbocharged.

So let me reassure you by sharing *my* target for every business I run. The one I throw a party to celebrate when we achieve it, because I think it's so important. **That target is zero.** It's achieved when a business is running at break-even: each month it brings in the same amount as it costs to run. It's no longer losing money. When you can get a business to zero, then it's real. It pays for itself, and if you keep going on the same trajectory, it will soon be making you money. Zero is the foundation for the house that you are trying to build. It says that the base is solid. You are nowhere near being finished, but you can trust in the thing you are creating.

Zero is not just an important goal for every new business. It's also a symbol of the importance of small successes, and how they add up over time. While I am the last person to tell people they shouldn't dream big, I'm also a strong advocate of thinking small when it comes to execution. You've got the dream out on the horizon—keeping you ambitious and reminding you of the plan you have for your life. But getting there doesn't mean you have to try and break the Olympic record every single day. I can't help ten million people with their dreams in a week, a year, or perhaps even a decade. But every day I can help a few people, who will help others, and over time that work will compound. Eventually I will reach the figure that is my dream, not by obsessing over it every day but by keeping it in the back of my mind and focusing most on what I can do *right now* to bring it closer.

You can—and should—go step by step. One small win at a time. **In my experience, that is how success and growth in business really happen. How dreams are achieved. Not through shortcuts or clever hacks, but by piling up your wins day by day, week by week, year by year.** As the saying goes, the man who wants to move a mountain first picks up one small rock.

And if you take this approach, targeting and treasuring all those wins, I can almost guarantee that before long you will be sailing past milestones that might once have intimidated you—or that could have tripped you up if you'd tried to achieve them in one go. Remember my 150 views? Four years later, I posted another video. It was nothing complicated: just me sitting at a table, talking for more than two hours about how to build a business. There were no gimmicks or giveaways. I didn't buy a supermarket or blow up a derelict factory. I just sat and talked, sharing the same kind of advice as I am in this book. After ten days, that video had been watched by 1.5 million people. (That's 999,900 percent growth for the people who like big numbers.)

Going from 150 to 1,500,000 symbolized a lot of things, but most of all the truth that what starts small can grow big. What feels like almost nothing at the beginning will compound over time until it is piled up in front of you, higher than you could have imagined. The acorn really does grow into the oak tree if you nurture it properly. That's why I urge you not to let other people define your success, especially in the early days of your business. Get wins on the board, celebrate them, hit zero, and keep going.

Grow with the customer you already have

One of the most tangible wins for any business is making a sale and landing a customer. Every entrepreneur is (rightly) motivated by the ringing of the till, whether you are actually running a shop or not. But there is also a danger here, because the pursuit of these wins can become so all-consuming that they actually *get in the way* of growing your business.

I often encounter this when advising people on how to grow a business they have built to a certain level. When people ask for my help, my first question is what do they think they need. And their answer, almost always, is more customers. That's a natural instinct, but it can be misguided. Note the emphasis on *more* customers. New customers.

But what about the ones you already have? In the constant pursuit of new customers, it's easy to forget about those who are already on your books. That is a combination of human nature and the way most businesses behave, rewarding people who bring in new business more than those who keep existing customers happy. Our hunter-gatherer instincts tell us to celebrate the ones who go off into new pastures and bring something back.

But although new is a powerful attraction, it isn't always best. That's a lesson I learned in the early days of Fluid. That business started with the client base that Helen had built up as a graphic designer. They were thrilled with her work, but she was undercharging them. When we agreed to go into business together, I might have seen those clients as a bad thing. They didn't want to pay what the work was worth. That made them a problem, didn't it?

But I already knew enough about business to know that those underpaying clients could still be an asset. So we persevered with them. I got to know them too. Soon their worth to us far outstripped the revenue we earned from their accounts. Those three clients became the foundation stone of our business: they became our advocates, they connected us to other customers, and they provided positive endorsements (an essential lesson for any early-stage business: never underestimate the power of a good customer reference).

One of the early customers those founding clients helped us to win was *Fortune* magazine. This was when magazines were still a big deal and had huge advertising revenue. We worked with *Fortune* on content, including advertorials for brands such as Aston Martin. Soon we were winning other work as a result, from some of those brands as well as *Fortune*'s parent company, CNN. Even better, *Fortune* became our most important reference. When I called people up, I was no longer Simon Squibb who worked for Fluid. I was Simon Squibb, who worked for clients such as *Fortune* magazine. My reference went from a name people had never heard of to one everyone was impressed by. This is a sales technique called selling the "sizzle" and not the steak. Don't just give a potential customer the bare facts—we design websites and develop marketing campaigns. Tell them the good part—in this case, if our work is good enough for *Fortune*, then it's good enough for your business too.

That is an example of how just one influential customer can be transformative for a business. Working for *Fortune* turned us from a nobody into a respected agency that was soon in a position to win high-profile clients and attract talent. The lesson is that your earliest customers will do a tremendous amount for your business if you treat them well. Someone who begins as a customer can quickly turn into your biggest advocate. That doesn't happen by accident. If you give a customer the outcome they wanted—a brilliant solution to their marketing problem, a shirt that actually fits them, a dog-walking or babysitting service they can rely on—then they won't keep it to themselves. They will tell their friends, colleagues, other parents at their kids' school.

Think about what you do when you discover something new, interesting, or useful. You tell people. You want to show off that you were the first to find out about this cool or helpful thing, and to put other people in on the secret. That is the kind of word-of-mouth marketing that money can't buy, and the only way you get it is by giving your customers such a good level of service that they *have* to talk to other people about it.

The importance of the customer and customer references is why I say that chasing new business can be dangerous. Not because getting more customers is a bad thing, but because there is a risk you will fall into the trap of believing that the only good business is new business. That in pursuit of the next customer, you will ignore your most loyal clients. This is a big mistake for several reasons. One is that any customer can tell when they are no longer the shiny new penny and being looked after as if they were the most important person in the world. Especially in a service business, like we were running at Fluid, clients quickly become unhappy when they sense that your attention has gone elsewhere and their business is no longer a priority.

The second reason is that looking after your best (and often most longstanding) customers is one of the best ways to grow your business. People forget this because they equate the growth of the business with the expansion of its customer base. They think you can only grow if you are selling to more customers each month. They believe that a new customer is worth more than an existing one. That can be true for certain types of business, but in many cases it is a dangerous oversimplification. It misses the crucial point that you generally grow through your biggest and most important customers, not at their expense.

In economics, there is a famous idea called the Pareto principle. In business terms, Pareto's principle says that 80 percent of the outcomes are generally produced by about 20 percent of the system. As in, you should expect your top 20 percent of salespeople to generate 80 percent of your sales, your top 20 percent of customers will be responsible for 80 percent of profit, and so on.

The numbers may not be exact, but the principle is a helpful one when it comes to thinking about customers and how to grow your business. If the vast majority of your success is going to come from just a fifth of your customer base, then you are going to be better off with an approach that goes deep rather than wide—trying to turn each client into one of the 20 percent that will spend more and more with you over time, refer you to new customers, and act as a brilliant advocate.

In other words, the *value* of your customer relationships is more important than the *volume*. Imagine you're running a window-cleaning business. If you do the job brilliantly for your first customer, take all the time it needs, and maybe even go a little further than what was expected or agreed, it won't be long before you have the entire street as customers. Whereas if you are rushing off to the next job halfway across town, perhaps leaving a few imperfect details, then you are not going to make the good impression that leads to repeat business, referrals, and all the things that help you grow. In this scenario, chasing the next customer may have cost you the previous one.

That's why your first priority should be looking after the customers you have, rewarding and reinforcing their loyalty. Those customers will not just pay your bills, they will point you to where your business should be expanding by telling you the problems they need help with, refer you to their friends, and say good things about you when you aren't in the room. Look after them right, and they will do almost as much to help grow the business as you do.

The customers you start a business with will often hold the key to the growth of your business. But they don't have all the answers. Your business mustn't forget its roots, nor can it stand still. Growth also means evolution: finding new ways to serve your customers, build your brand, and add revenue streams. Soon you will be in a position to hit the accelerator on growth, but first you must make sure you have the right foundations in place.

Get ready to grow

Earlier on I talked about how it might be a good idea to work for free if you believe that the client or customer could be worth more to you over the long term than the value of what you are selling right now. That is a valid approach that can pay you back many times over, but of course you cannot do it with each and every customer. You are in business to make some money, after all.

When it comes to the paying customers, which should be most of them, people think the key question is how much to charge. That's important, and you need to work out your pricing via a combination of the going rate in your industry and the amount of money you need to make the work profitable. But when it comes to bringing in money, the question of *when* is almost as important as *how much*.

This brings me to one of my absolute golden rules of

business: **ask for money upfront**. Please, please do this. If you are doing any kind of business that doesn't involve the customer paying in full at the point of purchase, you should always ask for a 50 percent deposit before beginning the work. That is partly about cashflow and your security as a business. But it's also about flexibility. If your pricing is right, that initial 50 percent will cover the costs of you doing the work in full. The second half will be pure profit—fuel for the growth of your business if you use it well.

This is exactly how we scaled up Fluid. The upfront payments we took from clients would cover our costs, and the remainder we invested in expansion. One of our biggest pieces of work in the early days was a brand development project. The second payment for that, the profit part, we used as seed capital to build an email marketing service—a software product that required investment to develop and that we couldn't have afforded to do at the start. That's how you bootstrap a business: begin with the things you can do cheaply or for free, make sure you get paid some money upfront, and invest the rest in growth.

There is also a good principle here: when bootstrapping a business, you **earn the right to grow**, generating the cash that can then be reinvested in systems, people, and new ideas. Earning that right can come in multiple forms, but the important thing is that you must build on a solid base. In some cases, that means you start by doing a business that seems boring, but will give you a brilliant foundation for growth and diversifying into the stuff you really want to do. Often the pathway to the dream may be through some unglamorous version of the same thing: like working as a music publicist to pay for making your own music, selling cars as a route to one day designing them, or working in advertising while writing a novel on the side.

This was the story of James and John, identical twins from Portsmouth who DM'd me one day, offering to clean the HelpBnk staircase as a way of promoting the cleaning business they wanted to start. When we spoke, I soon saw that they had a real dream with deep roots. The brothers, now in their early twenties, had had a tough life. They'd experienced homelessness in their teens and had not seen their dad for seventeen years—almost their entire lifetimes. He was living in a different country and, while they spoke all the time, they had not seen him except through a screen since first coming to the UK; the family had never been able to afford to bring him with them. These twins had pain and they had purpose. As they told me: "The only way we see our family coming together is if this business is successful."

The brothers had their dream, but they still needed to find a way of getting their business off the ground. They realized that if you just go around finding houses and offices to clean, you soon become another cleaning company like dozens of others in your local area. There is no reason for people to find or hire you instead of your competitors. When we talked about this problem while they were getting ready to launch the business, I suggested that they try to develop an eye-catching video format to boost their brand on social media. They went away and came up with the idea of cleaning the most dirty and dilapidated places they could find: passageways filled with junk, public toilets that smelled like hell, front gardens of unoccupied houses where people had been dumping their rubbish. James and John filmed themselves cleaning these places, they posted videos about it on social media, and they started using that content to promote their new commercial cleaning business. They introduce the videos with a catch-phrase I promise you won't be able to get out of your head once you've heard it: "I'm James, and I'm John, and we clean places *nobody* asked us to clean."

The reason this is such a good approach is that 1) it costs them nothing except their time to do; 2) it increases their profile and helps them to attract paid clients; and 3) if it continues to go well, it can build a brand that will allow them to do all sorts of things to generate additional revenue, like selling cleaning supplies to a much wider audience. Not to mention that if they grow their audience big enough, the content itself will start to make money. It's a great example of how you can use one part of a business to power another and turn an unglamorous business into an aspirational one. I think the twins' real future will be as content creators and influencers in the cleaning industry, but only because they were willing to start with the dirty, difficult, and unglamorous stuff—the actual cleaning work.

By contrast, I sometimes hear from people who seem to think that social media can be the silver bullet for their business, helping them to find the customers they are otherwise struggling to attract. One important thing to remember is that social media can be a brilliant tool, but it may also be a distraction. If you're using it smartly and it's helping you to grow or diversify your business, as in the case of James and John, then all power to you. But if you are putting time into social media at the expense of the core of your business, stop and think again.

An important lesson at the beginning of your business journey is to play to your strengths and **do the basics well** before you start playing with bells and whistles. Let's go back to the window-cleaning example: if you're starting this business, don't waste time sitting in front of the computer editing content. Go out and look for expensive homes with dirty windows. Knock on their doors, clean some windows, and ask your happy clients to recommend you to their neighbors and friends. Offer to clean gutters and do other related jobs to give you secondary income. Then, once you have got that engine up and running, scaled up with several people working for you, maybe think about trying to build a brand online that will allow you to further diversify and grow your business.

Doing the basics well and generating cash by taking payment upfront are the absolute pillars of any new business. Get those in place and soon you will be in a position to do more interesting things, looking for growth in new and unexpected places, breaking new ground for your business. Now you are ready to go faster and begin the hunt for growth.

Hunting for growth

I still remember the conversation and where it took place. It was about a year into Fluid's life as a company and we were doing pretty well. We'd won *Fortune* and the flywheel was beginning to turn. We could see how the business would grow if we kept our standards high and our people happy. But there was still a lingering dissatisfaction. Like any agency business, our life was in the hands of our clients. They could walk away, cancel work, or demand substantial revisions at any moment. To a significant extent, we were reliant on their goodwill.

Helen and I were discussing this one evening in a bar. On the table in front of me was a small stack of beer mats. I'd been pushing one from side to side for about half an hour as we talked shop and debated what we could do differently. Then the idea dropped like a penny clattering into the bottom of my glass. I hadn't just been playing with the coaster, I'd been looking at it—reading it. These coasters weren't just something to rest your drink on. They were an advertising medium. And a much better one than the billboards you walk by or the bus ads that flash past you on the street. Because when people sit down at a bar table, they probably stay for an hour or even several. That is the definition of a captive audience.

I held it up. "Why don't we make these?"

It was a simple idea but, at the time, no one was doing it. We would make coasters, sell them as advertising space—like mini billboards—to brands and then work with venues to get them placed in bars and restaurants across Hong Kong. It was an attractive concept for several reasons: as a design company, we could manage the creative in-house, and already had good experience in helping brands, to tell a story through advertising. More than that, this would be a different type of business, one where we would sell a product rather than being hired as a service provider. As an extension to our business, it was rooted in things we already did well, but at the same time it took us into new territory we wanted to occupy: owning our own product and the revenue associated with it.

Just as I have advised you to, we effectively set up this business for free. Because I had never sold advertising space before, I called up billboard companies and got them to explain their rate cards to me: how they justified charging a certain amount for displaying an advert for a particular period of time, in a defined location. When we learned that the costs are explained by eyeballs (or in technical terms, OTS—opportunity to see), we literally stood outside bars and restaurants counting people in and out, so we could present potential clients with a realistic projection of how many people might sit in front of that coaster on a given evening. Then we approached the venues and got their buy-in: a revenue share in return for agreeing to use our coasters in place of those provided by the drinks companies. Finally, I went and pitched the idea for what we called

CoasterAds to twenty major brands, promising exclusivity to the first advertiser for six months.

That customer was United Airlines. They became the founding client of CoasterAds and soon we had devised a campaign where they placed newspaper ads encouraging people to go to one of the participating bars, pick up a coaster, and apply to win a free vacation. What had begun as an idle thought in a bar had quickly turned into a business that benefited everyone involved: the client got the exposure they wanted, by tapping into the customer base of the upmarket venues we had negotiated placements with; the venues not only made money for nothing through the revenue share, but also benefited from free advertising via the United campaign. It was a win-win. And Helen and I had invested nothing except our time.

The contract with United specified that they would pay 50 percent upfront, which covered all our costs in creative, printing, and distribution. Once the campaign had been delivered, the rest of the fee was pure profit, allowing us to invest in the growth of the business. We'd even gotten both the CoasterAds and Fluid names into the creative, which led to inbound inquiries for our main business.

Within a year, CoasterAds was bringing in as much revenue as Fluid, and by the time we sold it, it had made millions in profit. This was a business we had set up for free, bootstrapped into a multimillion valuation, and used as a platform to promote the work of the company we already had. It showed that the growth of a business doesn't always happen in a straight line. Success isn't necessarily about doing more of what you are already doing. To grow, you might need to diversify your business or strike an interesting partnership. Ask yourself: is there something that many of my customers need that I could be providing; are there ways I could be getting more out of my network and brand; are there channels I haven't considered distributing through?

Almost every business has unrealized potential in one form or another. That might be obvious, like a clothing brand deciding to do sweatshirts as well as T-shirts, or an ice cream business starting to cater corporate events. Or it might require some lateral thinking, as in the case of Fluid, where we had thought of ourselves as a purely creative agency, and realized we also had the potential to operate as a media company that could occupy an innovative niche.

Of course, there is a balance to strike here: not every idea is going to be a million-dollar business waiting to happen. Some attempts to diversify are going to lead you down dead ends. Others may go somewhere, but end up being more distraction than valuable addition. We found this out to our cost later on, when a subsequent attempt at branching out went wrong. In 2007, with the business in good health, we opened our own café in the same building as our office. We called it Graze and imagined it functioning both as a place for our team to hang out (with discounted prices) and as a profitable business that would attract the general public as customers. Over time, we believed it was a model we might be able to roll out more widely: a coffee shop that was halfway between the workplace and the outside world.

But unlike CoasterAds, which effectively plugged straight into our existing business, a café could not be spun up out of nowhere and at almost zero cost. We had to invest in fitting out a space and hiring people who knew the food and beverage industry. We were dealing with the costs and slippages that are part and parcel of running a hospitality business: credit card payments that took ninety days to arrive, glasses getting broken, food being wasted. Although the café was mostly busy, we struggled to make any money from it. We were out of our comfort zone and eventually realized that we weren't running an extension of our existing business but a completely separate one. Graze had become a distraction, it wasn't reliably profitable, and we shut it down. It took us five years to realize that, though, and I'd love it if this book could save you that pain by understanding that you need to diversify smartly, in ways that play to your strengths and where you have the business equivalent of home advantage.

I'm far from the only entrepreneur to have learned this difficult lesson. I once interviewed Pip Murray, founder of Pip & Nut, a hugely successful range of natural peanut and almond butters, now sold by thousands of retailers around the country. It was the classic entrepreneurial success story, from the kitchen table to sales in the multimillions within a handful of years. Then Pip decided to diversify into nut "mylk"—a milk substitute—trying to capitalize on the trend for healthy vegan lifestyles. On the face of it, this made sense: if the brand could have huge success with one range of nut-based products, why not another? But, as Pip told me, it was a disaster: the manufacturing process was very different from the core product, the position in the shops was less favorable, and the competitive landscape was brutal. It didn't work and she quickly shut it down. What had seemed like a small sideways step in fact became an unmanageable jump.

These are examples of how going for growth can mislead you: when what seems like a viable extension of your brand becomes a pit into which you sink time and money with little meaningful return. Our experience with Graze was a reminder not to stray too far from what made us successful in the first place. But we were not daunted by that failure, and you should not be put off challenging yourself in search of growth.

There will come a time when you want, and probably need, to expand your focus and take your business in new directions. As long as you have a solid operation in place and won't be taking your eye off the ball, there is limited cost to these experiments and potentially a huge benefit. You don't grow a business without taking some risks and daring to be creative. Keep coming up with new ideas, add bubbles to your mind map, and when your gut tells you that you have to try one of them, then give it a go. Even if you fail, you will learn something and be better placed to get the next extension or expansion of your brand right.

Invest in success

"Growth is never by mere chance; it is the result of forces working together."

This is a quote I love from a brilliant entrepreneur, James Cash Penney, who created the American department store chain JCPenney.

What are those forces, and how can you harness them in your favor?

As we've already noted, perhaps the first and most important force is the customer. If you follow the customer, meet and exceed their needs, and nurture a loyal relationship over time, you will be repaid many times over. Remember the Pareto principle: your top 20 percent of customers will do more business with you over time, they will connect you to other clients, and they will help to build your brand by speaking well of you. Every good business creates satisfied customers, who provide much of its most important marketing.

The next force is your own people. We will talk more in the

next chapter about how to find and nurture brilliant people, who are the driving force of any business. But safe to say, your business is not going to grow unless you really look after your people and get them as enthused in the success of the company (and the dream it is helping you to achieve) as you are.

That's why I say you have to **invest in success at the growth stage**. By this point, you have worked out your business model. You know you are not throwing good money after bad. You can afford the expensive podcast studio, not just the crappy Amazon microphone. And you will benefit from that investment, which will help you to produce a higher quality product. It's at this point that you need to give yourself permission to invest back in the business. Pay good people more and give them equity. Choose a beautiful office that people will want to work in and outfit it properly (or ensure their home office has everything it needs). Invest in the equipment and systems you need to go to the next level. Above all else, ensure that you give your people freedom and flexibility in how and where they work.

As we discussed, you need to act poor at the beginning of your business journey, even if you have money to burn. Hold on to every penny and spend only what you must. But that equation *flips on its head* once you are established and trying to grow. At this point, you will drive people away if you try to bargain them down on salary and incentives or make them work in inferior conditions. And you will deter potential customers and investors if you aren't investing fully in your digital presence and all the places people can find your brand.

Not long ago, a company pitched me for investment. When I went on their website and social media channels, I found multiple links that were outdated and a news section where the last post was six months old. It was a classic example of how you should do things properly or not do them at all. Better no website than a poorly maintained one. At this level of maturity as a business, anything with your brand on it will be taken as representative. If any visible part of your business appears broken, people will assume that everything must be and they will quickly look elsewhere. That's why you will hamstring your business if you don't invest in the right infrastructure as you grow and hire the right people to maintain it. In the same way that you need to start a business poor, you should aspire to grow it rich.

How do you do this? You need to follow one of the most important principles I have learned in business: **when you make money from your company, don't take it off the table**. Don't use it to buy yourself a house or go on a long-deserved vacation. Instead, invest that money back into the business. Give out pay raises, improve your premises, develop and market your brand. I can guarantee that you will see a return on that investment over the long term, when it comes time to take money out of the business through selling a stake in it, or the entire operation. Whereas if you are nibbling away at the profits while running the business, paying for a new house or your next vacation, you will undermine your growth and the value of your eventual return. Those who practice delayed gratification will be most successful in the long run.

As well as investing money the business makes back into growth, you may want to consider taking on outside investment at this stage. This is perhaps the most frequent question I am asked: Simon, how do I get an investor?

To which my response is always: are you sure you need an investor? A lot of people assume that third-party investment is by definition a good thing, signifying that you have "made it" as a business. But I can promise you that if you get the wrong investor, or take investment for the wrong reasons, then it will ruin your life. The thrill of getting the money will soon wear off, and you will find yourself effectively working for someone you wish you had never met. If you're not careful, your shiny new investor can very quickly become the nightmare boss you thought you'd escaped when you quit your last job.

If you are sure that you do want an investor, then think carefully about where to find them. At an early stage when the sums are relatively small, consider raising money from family and friends if appropriate. These are people who already know you and want you to succeed. The only thing to remember is that you mustn't oversell. Don't jeopardize close personal relationships for the sake of the business.

If family and friends aren't available, then at the early stage you are probably looking for an angel investor. These are individuals with personal wealth who invest in businesses, often entrepreneurs who have sold their own businesses (this is how I invest). They have the ability to write a check and the knowledge and experience to give you hands-on support with building your business. You can find angels by getting involved with business networks, pitching your company at events, or simply getting to know other founders and asking them to introduce you to their investors.

But remember: you're not looking for an angel investor but *the* investor who is right for your business. One who believes in your purpose, has relevant expertise, and who you think you will be happy to spend a lot of time working with. People think investors are the ones who get to be picky, but founders should be equally careful when looking for funding. Seek out the best investors for your business: tell them not that you are looking to raise money, but that you are looking to raise money from the right people. Explain how you think that they (and they in particular) can help you to grow and develop the business. Remember that you are building this business to achieve your dream, not so you can end up working for yet another boss who happens to call themselves an investor. Be selective. And remember my golden rule of investment: **if you ask for money, you'll get advice, and if you ask for advice, you'll (probably) get money**.

At later stages, other investors may be appropriate, such as venture capital (VC). But be aware that these are specialist investment firms that are looking for companies that can grow very big, very quickly. They want to find the next Airbnb, Lululemon, or Five Guys. If your ambitions are that big and you can show massive traction and growth potential in your business, then you might be able to get a VC interested. If so, then again you have to do your due diligence: find a firm that is relevant to the sector you are in, look at the other companies they have invested in, and ideally get someone to introduce you.

A final way to seek investment, which people rarely talk about, is from people you hire into the business. Sometimes you reach a point where you know that you need a certain quality of hire or level of experience, but are worried you won't be able to attract that person to your company. They are already working for a bigger competitor, almost certainly on a bigger salary than you can afford to pay them. Often that is the Number Two person, who effectively runs the company on behalf of a CEO or founder. They might seem out of reach, so how do you recruit them? Quite simply, you offer them something their current employer never will: a major ownership stake. You invite them literally to buy into the company. This way, you can potentially kill two birds with one stone: you get the hire you really wanted and the funding you needed at the same time.

However and whenever you go about seeking investment, the rules are basically the same. Find the right person, tell them why you are the right business for them as an investor, and ask for their help before you ask for their money. Look for someone who can add value to your business and will be happy that you gave them the chance to invest. I promise that no one is going to sit on a comfy chair berating you: *Dragons' Den* is not real life. But if you find the right investors, who are aligned with your purpose, it can make a huge difference and allow you to move more quickly and take more ambitious steps.

After customers, people, and investors, the final force for growth is you. It was you, the founder of the business, who helped to give it life in the first place. And it is your actions that will determine how successfully that business grows over time. Part of this is about the things you do. You are still the person who is best placed to set the direction of the business, whether that is seeing new opportunities to expand, managing important client relationships, or winning new business. And as the founder, you also have the most opportunity to color outside the lines and do something unexpected or opportunistic. Sniffing out opportunities and agreeing to invest time (and sometimes money) in them is part of the founder's job.

At the same time, you also have to know what *not* to do. For most entrepreneurs, this is the hard part. You are used to doing things and making decisions. Action has served you well. But past a certain point, you can't do it all on your own. And if you try, then you are going to hold back the very people you have recruited to help you grow the business.

I encounter this a lot. People say they are finding it difficult to scale their business. They are stuck and they're struggling to grow. If this is your problem, then I have news for you. You need to take a look in the mirror. Like it or not, you are almost certainly the one impeding the growth of your own business.

Let me explain how this works. You've built the business up from nothing and been the primary driver of success. You're still the one who brings in most new business. You're still probably the biggest rainmaker on your team. It couldn't happen without you. The problem is that everyone knows this and they act accordingly. They don't feel empowered to take decisions without checking with you first. Subconsciously, they know that they are not expected to step up and take more responsibility. If there is a problem or you are at risk of not hitting that month's target, they are going to look to you to make up the shortfall.

That is not their shortcoming but yours. Your shadow within the business is too large and, like plants that live in the shade, your people are not getting the chance to grow. This is commonly known as founder syndrome, where the person who started the business retains too great a role at a point when success should be resting on many more shoulders.

It's a problem that only the founder can solve, and you do it through the three T's—**train people, trust people, and tear yourself away**. I learned this at Fluid, when after a few years of running the business I had the idea that only I was capable of doing the important jobs. I thought I had to be leading every pitch, handling every major client, and representing the business at every industry event. It took some time to realize that, by doing so, I was both harming myself and holding back my great team.

At this point, I sat down and wrote a list of all the things I was doing. I literally broke down my job and started handing out pieces of it. I trained people I knew were talented to take up roles they hadn't previously been comfortable with. I trusted people who already deserved to have more responsibility. And I tore myself away from the business. I was still the CEO, and I still did lots of pitching, client handling, and networking. But I no longer felt that the business might fail without me. I took a step back so that others could step up and the business could surge forward, which is exactly what happened.

That sums up how growth is a tricky thing for any business: a mixture of things you need to do, things you need not to do, and all the usual accidents of luck and timing. There are lots of important aspects to it, so in the chapters that follow we'll look at each of these in turn, from the team you need to build around you, to the risk-taking ability you must hone, the perseverance you must demonstrate, and the self-awareness you must show to manage and evolve your own role.

We start with perhaps the most important growth enabler of all: the people and partnerships who can take your business to the next level.

10.

Find Brilliant People

During my career, I have hired hundreds of people as employees and gone into business with dozens. I've had brilliant people work for me, and others where it was clear on the first day that a mistake had been made. I've started business partnerships that have endured for decades, and others where people have brazenly ripped me off. I've done deals that made me more money than I will ever need, and others that have seen large investments go up in smoke.

All of those good and bad experiences have convinced me of one thing above all. **The people you do business with matter more than almost anything else.** The success or failure of your company is going to rest in large part on your ability to hire (and fire) well, to strike good partnerships, to find the right investors and advisors. It's going to depend on how good you are at bringing the right people into the tent with you and keeping the wrong ones out.

That last bit may sound harsh, but there is no getting away from the fact that bad people can break your business as much as good ones can help to make it. People who aren't aligned with your dream, who don't share your purpose or moral code, and who don't have a strong motivation to succeed are going to be a big problem on your business journey.

By the same token, great people will surprise you with

how much they can do and how important they can be. They will save you from mistakes, see opportunities you had missed, and help you to drive the business forward. Before long, they will be running the show as well if not better than you can, as long as you reward and look after them properly.

The importance of the people you work with grows along with your business. You won't just need more people as you get bigger, you'll also need different kinds of skills and possibly to change the way you hire. You may choose to take on outside investment or to strike partnerships to fuel your growth, which opens up a whole new category of people where you must choose carefully. You may want to nurture not just a customer base, but a community that is aligned with the purpose of your business, supports the dream it is working towards, and helps to supercharge both things.

Ask any entrepreneur about their biggest challenge and most will say people. It's the hardest, most time-consuming task and no amount of systems or sophistication can save you from having to make individual decisions about who you want to work with. It's impossible to get every one of those decisions right, but you can improve your chances by having a process and knowing the main pitfalls to avoid. That's why I am devoting this chapter to sharing my knowledge about how to pick partners, how to hire and fire employees, and how to build communities. Because while your dream may be personal, you are only going to achieve it if you get enough of the right people to share it and come on the journey with you. Teamwork does in fact make the dream work.

How to pick partners

Probably the first person you will need to find, and definitely the most important, is a business partner.

When you get it right, a business partnership can be an amazing thing. The most significant of my career was, of course, with Helen. When we first met, she was an underpaid graphic designer. I was still sleeping on my friend's sofa, trying to justify my move to Hong Kong, and she was more interested in dating another of my friends than me. We had a laugh debating names for the business idea we were discussing, including Pink Tank (on the basis you would definitely look twice at a logo with that image on it). But I don't think either of us would have guessed then that we'd go on to run a successful business together for the next fifteen years, get married, and become parents together.

Unfortunately, not all business partnerships are destined to be so fruitful. In my career, I have experienced what it is like to work with cofounders who were not who they pretended to be, who lost interest in the business over time, or who had a fundamentally different idea from me about what direction to go in. I have learned from those mishaps and, in retrospect, can see how I could have avoided many of those situations. When making decisions about partnerships today, I am much more rigorous about assessing whether a relationship is likely to work and why. I have a process, which I will share with you here.

But first, you may be asking, do I really need a partner? Isn't it my dream, and shouldn't I be the one responsible for it? Can't I start and run this business on my own? The simple answer is: yes, of course you can. Some people prefer to work alone and that's fine. Jeff Bezos didn't have a cofounder at

Amazon, nor did Nick Jenkins, founder of Moonpig, who told me the worst thing in the world for him would be to have a cofounder, because he loved the autonomy of making all the decisions on his own.

Perhaps the more truthful answer is that you *can* go it alone, but you might not want to. There are real benefits to having someone (and perhaps several people) running the show with you. It's a bit like going to the gym: of course you can establish a successful habit and make gains entirely on your own, but for many people it will be easier if you have one or more gym buddies. They encourage you to go when you don't feel like it, they hold you accountable to your goals and, most importantly, they make it more fun.

Business partners offer those advantages and more. They can also help to balance out any skills or experience you lack. If you are not a technical person, or a numbers person, or even a people person, then someone who thrives in those areas may be exactly the cofounder you need. It will allow you each to focus on different areas of the business, contributing in ways the other cannot.

Having a partner also provides the kind of counterbalance that nobody can provide for themselves. However much we think we know, ours is just one opinion, one set of experiences, one bundle of biases. Most of us don't know what we don't know: having a partner is one of the best ways to broaden your mind and challenge your assumptions. Often it will help you to make better and more rounded decisions.

Assuming you want a partner, how do you find one? Just like when you identified your ideal customer, the first thing is to know *exactly* what and who you are looking for. This may sound obvious or even flippant, but I promise you it's important and will pay dividends. Write down a description of the person you would like to go into business with. Be as detailed as you can: where do they come from, what have they been doing for the last two years, what age are they? Ask yourself: if there was one person in the world you could run this business with and pursue your dream alongside, who would it be? Trying to imagine the person you will work with is not some woo-woo manifestation exercise. It's the simple psychology that we generally see what we are already looking for. If I talk to you about red cars for five minutes, I promise you will spend the rest of the day noticing them.

Once you have defined your parameters, go looking for that person. There are lots of ways, but the most efficient is simply to tell people that you are starting a business and looking for a cofounder. Post about it online. Tell your friends and colleagues. You are not going to find the right copilot for your business unless you make it clear that you are looking.

Let's say that works and you have found a potential partner: perhaps it arose in conversation that a friend of yours was also wavering in their job and thinking about starting a business. Or they knew a friend, sister-in-law, or ex-colleague who might be the perfect partner for you. How do you know that a person is right? How do you judge whether or not to trust your dream to someone?

My test for potential business partners is twofold: we need to have the right things in common *and* the right things that make us different. **Instinctively, we look for the similarities, but in a partnership differences matter just as much.** Combining two identical people is not the ideal recipe for a business: it's like having two left hands, or two people trying to play the same position on a sports team. You will get in each other's way and not cover each other's weaknesses. It's on "hard" factors—skills, experience, knowledge—that you ideally want a few degrees of difference. You should excel at looking after one area of a business while your partner takes care of another. This is the case for many tech start-ups, which often pair a "technical" cofounder with one who is more focused on hiring, marketing, and everything that doesn't involve writing code.

But for all those differences, you need at least one thing in common. This is important and you should never enter a business partnership without it. **You need to share a moral code.** You have to believe in the same fundamental principles about how to treat people and do business. However exceptional two founders may be, if they have different ideas about how to remunerate their staff, treat their customers, or honor contractual terms, those are going to prove irreconcilable over the long term.

The nature of a business partnership is that while you might have different areas of focus day to day, you will make the big and difficult decisions together. It's those decisions that reveal whether you share a moral code: a basic sense of the right and wrong way to do things.

A good example came during the 2008 financial crisis. As a major banking center, Hong Kong was hit hard and business quickly took a turn for the worse. Helen and I watched as our clients began to shut up shop and our competitors quickly laid off staff. It seemed like we had no choice but to follow suit. If Fluid was to survive, we would have to reduce our staff and try to ride out the storm. One day I said as much to Helen: either we started laying people off or the company would die.

Yet something stopped us from doing it. We couldn't bring ourselves to cast adrift many brilliant people who had helped to build the business with us, at a time when we knew there was no other work for them. Both of us shared a view that layoffs were the right thing to do logically and the wrong one morally. Helen summed it up when she said to me: "If the company dies, we can always just do something else." That settled it: we would fight to save both the company and all the people in it. Rather than announcing layoffs, we did something counterintuitive. We started hiring, knowing that great talent had been let go from our competitors. We decided to try and grow our way out of trouble.

It was a big risk and it might not have worked. At times, it looked like we were going to run out of cash. But in the event, the financial crisis did not affect our local market for as long as people had expected. Business started to bounce back and we were ready to take advantage, equipped with more great people (and in many cases their clients) than before.

The gamble had paid off, though it might not have done had the crisis gone on for even a few more months. But the important thing was that Helen and I had been united in pursuing this approach, after my initial wobble. It had grown out of a shared moral code about how to treat people. We had both known that, for us, trying to save ourselves at the expense of our staff was not a decision we could live with. That is what I mean when I say there will be a big decision that reveals whether you are aligned with your business partner on morals and values. Those are the things you need to have in common if your partnership is going to hold together when it comes under stress.

If you find someone you share both a dream and a code with, I promise you it can be one of the most significant and meaningful relationships of your life. Partnership is not easy, but it is almost always worth the effort. Done right, it makes building your business half as difficult and twice as fun.

How to hire people

Most businesses can be started without employees, but very soon you reach the limit of what a founding team can do alone. You can't run a business with the left hand and grow it with the right. You need people. My basic principle of scaling up any business is that every time you hire someone good, life gets a little easier.

Hiring and managing people can be both the best and worst part of running a business. When it goes well, your company benefits and you get the satisfaction of helping someone to further their career. Some of the best relationships you form will be with people who started off working for you, and then went on to great things afterwards—you might become their customer later, or an investor in their business. But on the flip-side, when it goes badly, it feels like whole days are lost trying to deal with that person's problems. These are cases where it seems like neither you nor they can do anything right. It was always the wrong hire, and the only question is how both sides can extricate themselves from the mess.

How, then, do you hire in a way that maximizes your chances of finding people in the first group? It starts with something we've already discussed and which I know you now have. It starts with purpose. My experience in business has been that hiring well is hard when you lack a purpose other than to make money, and it becomes fairly easy once you have found a purpose and organized your business around it.

That purpose provides a litmus test for whether people are really interested in being part of your business, and it acts as a galvanizing force for the team you are building. If you have it, then you will spend much more time managing purpose than you do people—focusing on the collective ethos of your organization. **If you lack purpose, then you are going to have a group of individuals, not a proper team.** People will be focused on themselves because you have given them nothing to rally around. The result is that you will spend almost every day dealing with some kind of personal problem or complaint.

Having purpose is one thing, but how do you use it to hire the right people? Alignment with purpose is one of my hiring criteria, but of course anyone can pay lip service to an idea and sound convincing during an interview. You have to look deeper to see if potential hires really mean what they say. One part of this is simple diligence—to check that the person who says they are deeply committed to the environment isn't posting about gas guzzlers on their socials.

Another is a test of commitment. Say I am hiring for a video editor. I will put out an ad on social media and interview the most promising candidates. Then I will ask the best ones if they are willing to edit my next video as part of the interview process (i.e., without being paid). Some people don't want to do this, which I understand, but I find that people who believe in our purpose are happy to show what they are capable of. They really want the job and are happy to invest in the hiring process. For me that is a small test of commitment and alignment. How interested are you? Is this the job you really want, or just one out of a dozen applications? Why would you want to hire someone who sees you as interchangeable? I certainly don't treat the people I hire like this: each of them is working in the business because they share its purpose, it will help them with their career (and their own aspirations to run a business one day), and I trust them enough to give them equity. It reflects my belief that good hiring is about employees and employers who both make a positive choice to choose and show commitment to each other.

If you can find someone who appears to have that commitment, and who buys into your purpose, then there is one final test. One of the most important questions I use in any interview.

Let me try it out on you.

Here's a hypothetical offer. I will give you everything you have ever wanted. Riches and reputation, possessions and purpose, fame and family. A picture postcard of the perfect life. You can live in this paradise from whatever age you currently are until your seventieth birthday. At this point, it will be revealed that you are a fraud. You cheated people and ruined their lives. You are the new Bernie Madoff. Until you turn seventy, nobody will know this. As soon as you do, everyone will.

The question is simple: do you accept the offer?

In response, I would say people split almost perfectly down the middle. Half say yes and half no. I don't think the ones who want to take the deal are bad people, but I do think they are misguided about what success looks like and how it is achieved. I think they have never been properly educated about the importance of ethics and a moral code. And I don't think they are the right people to be working in my businesses.

A good rule of thumb in business is that the faster you rise, the quicker you fall. Remember Sam Bankman-Fried, the crypto whizz-kid? Almost overnight, his on-paper wealth grew to over $25 billion. Then, in the blink of an eye, he was being put on trial, found guilty, and sentenced to a twenty-five-year prison term. For 99.9 percent of cases, the idea of getting rich quickly and easily is either a fraud or a mirage.

That's why I ask the question (though by putting it in this

book, I will now have to find another one). It tests out how realistic people are about how success is achieved and what is to come. It also acts as a check on moral code. Does this person want to do things the right way, or are they willing to cut corners? In the end, your personal brand is all you have: you have to value your reputation above all else.

The option to cut corners may seem enticing, but it is also asking for trouble. In the very early days of Fluid, I was hiring for a marketing role and interviewed someone who was working for one of our main competitors. His pitch to me wasn't about skills or experience, but a more direct appeal to my self-interest. This person ran the client database for my competitor. He offered, in effect, to bring it with him and turn a huge amount of commercially sensitive information over to us. Exploiting it would transform our business. We could be bigger than the competitor within a year or two, rather than the decade or more it would otherwise take.

It was an easy decision. I rejected the offer, not just because it had gone against my moral code, and that I knew that to accept it would take us into dubious legal territory. I also didn't want to build my business by taking shortcuts. By the time we had exited Fluid, I was proud of the fact that we had spent fifteen years building that company. It was an achievement to be proud of and I never had to question if we had done things the right way. Nor did I want to bring anyone into the company who might undermine that intention without me knowing about it. Say I had hired the person who wanted to rip off his previous employer: even if I had been comfortable with the deal that was being offered, how could I have been sure that he would not end up doing the same thing to us when he wanted to leave?

It comes down to knowing the kind of people you want to

bring into your business. In many ways, you want to build a very diverse team: people with different backgrounds, different ages and life experiences, different skills and interests. But in a few key areas—namely purpose, mission, and moral code—you will come to regret any lack of alignment.

That's why it's so important to choose your people carefully and hire for the right reasons—not simply because someone comes well recommended, has relevant experience, or is readily available. At HelpBnk, I exclusively hire people who have either run their own business before or who I know are likely to do so one day. That is my test for having a team of motivated, free-thinking people who share the purpose of helping people to achieve their dreams and build their own businesses. I know that most of those people will eventually leave, probably to run their own companies. They will go with my blessing and, very likely, my investment. But for now, they are exactly the people I need to pursue this dream, and they can do it while gaining the experience that will help them move closer to their own.

Working out how to hire well for your business can take time. Mistakes are inevitable and you will have to learn and evolve. In the early days of Fluid, I believed the right approach was to hire young graduates who were untainted by the experience of working at my larger competitors. I wanted people who we could mold in our way of doing business. We found some great people this way, but kept running into the same problem. After a few years, those people mostly chose to go and work for our competitors. They wanted to know what it would be like to work for a bigger, more established name. The exact reason I had hired them—their lack of corporate experience—was the same one that led many to leave. So we adapted and started hiring more people who had done a couple of years at the bigger firms and were jaded by the experience. That proved a more sustainable approach over the long term.

As your business grows, you may also need to change the kind of employees you hire. In a start-up with a very small team, it helps to have people who can do a bit of everything. Great all-rounders will help you to plug gaps and to make up for the fact that you lack depth. Whereas at scale, you will often need to switch the emphasis from generalists to specialists. As a more mature organization, you need people who are brilliant at the thing they do, rather than those who can try their hand at most things. You scale a business by making it run more efficiently, which generally means having more different disciplines run by people who can do their job as quickly and capably as possible. You don't want the same person who cleans the windows managing the fleet of vehicles, doing the accounts, and running the sales team. Those are specialist jobs that require specialist skills.

However you do it, hiring great people is only the beginning. Holding on to them is just as important. People will tell you that this is complicated and difficult, but in my experience it isn't. It just involves doing something that a lot of entrepreneurs don't want to do: breaking up their ownership stake in the company and giving people a piece. **Let me say that again. If you want good people to stay at your company, then you need to give them equity.** This is an incredibly simple point that a lot of people try to talk around, simply because they don't like the answer. They say they pay well, give out bonuses, offer great incentives, and have a strong culture.

That's great, and you should do all that, but none of it comes close to giving people actual ownership of the value they create. Remember that these are the people making sales on your behalf, doing deals, and managing finances. They know how the business is doing and the role they played in its success. Anything short of giving them an actual share in that success is going to leave them feeling shortchanged. Whereas the knowledge that they will be compensated through a share in the business itself, not just their salary and perks, both rewards them for what they have done and provides an incentive for them to keep helping you build the business. Remember: ownership conveys freedom. You wanted it for yourself, and you are not a good boss if you try to deny it to the people you hired to grow your business.

That does not mean you have to give everyone a 5 percent stake of the company in their welcome pack. The way you deliver this will differ according to your circumstances. There are various approaches, from direct equity ownership to handing out share options that give people the right to buy shares at a certain price, after a certain time. Some companies might prefer a profit-sharing arrangement to one that concerns equity ownership. And you might only want to give equity to people who have stuck with you for a certain amount of time. But however you manage it, you need to find a way of sharing the actual proceeds and value of the business with the people who create it. You need to talk openly about it and show people what the path to ownership is if they don't already have it. And you need to kill the idea that sharing out equity is tantamount to giving up control and ownership of your business.

I often hear people saying that to do this is some huge risk. What if people leave and walk away with a slice of your company? To which my immediate answer is that of course people will sometimes leave, and in my experience if you have hired well, then you can always come to a reasonable agreement about buying back their equity if that is the right solution.

More generally, you have to ask yourself: what is the bigger risk? Losing some ownership over the company, or having your best assets—your people—walk out of the door because they don't feel valued? Do you want to own 100 percent of a company that's struggling because of high staff turnover, or 51 percent of one that is thriving because its best people are fully committed to the job and working every day to try to grow the business? The answer should be obvious, underlining that few things matter more in business than finding the right people and doing whatever it takes to keep them working with you.

How to fire people (or why 7 + 8 = trouble)

"If you hire well enough, you will never have to fire anyone."

I wish that statement were true, but it's not. However experienced you are at recruiting people, and however rigorous your process may be, the fact is that if you hire enough people, at least a few of them will not work out. It might not be their fault or yours. This could be the wrong job, the wrong time, the wrong place. But the fact remains that they are a failed hire, and you need to do something about it. Firing people is a necessary skill as a business owner, and you need to learn how to do it. Anyone who says otherwise is being hopelessly naive.

This isn't just for your benefit and that of the business. Long experience has taught me that many people who are underperforming in their job are secretly looking for a way out of it. They either can't or don't want to do the job. Don't laugh when I say that you are doing this person a favor by terminating them. Enough people have thanked me later for firing them, because it was the spur they needed to find success and fulfillment elsewhere. In some cases, I was able to help that person find another role that suited them better. A potentially unhappy situation turned into a win-win.

You can only manage that if you take a clearheaded view towards your people. You need to know exactly where people stand and to be honest with them and yourself. A lot of business owners don't do this. They hope the problem of an underperforming staff member will go away without the need for interventions and awkward conversations. They try to rationalize the situation and pretend that the person is not really doing so badly. They pray for a miracle. And they are always disappointed, because they end up having to get involved much later in the process, when the problem has become more entrenched.

This arises from what I call the rule of seven and eight. In your business, it shouldn't be hard to know where most people rank on a basic scale of one to ten. Anyone at or below a six is obviously struggling. It isn't a tough decision to move them on, provided you have taken all the necessary legal steps. They know and you know that it isn't working.

Then you have the nines and tens, your star performers who make the business what it is and excel at almost any challenge you throw at them. With these people, your biggest fear is that they may choose to leave. Hence the need to give them equity, look after them, and reward their contribution.

Where it gets complicated is with people who rank at either seven or eight out of ten. The people who fall right in between the high and low performers. They might be a nine on a good day, and a four on a bad one. They are people who can do the job, but who can't necessarily be relied upon. Who might follow instructions but have no willingness to take initiative. Who are often steady but show little sign of wanting or trying to improve.

It is in managing sevens and eights that so many business owners get it wrong. Sometimes they think they can help these people to become a consistent nine. Or they reason that it's too big a risk to fire someone who's not terrible at their job, because what if you can't replace them? The upshot is that many good businesses suffer because they hold on to people who aren't quite good enough to be there.

This is why you need to know the rule of seven and eight. It's this: **if you keep these people, then the nines and tens will leave**. When you accept and endorse people who are not performing at the highest standard, the best employees on your team will think that you do not fully value their contribution. They will see people they know are not as good as them getting equivalent rewards. And they will decide to go somewhere that takes them more seriously. By avoiding what felt like a tough decision—firing a "seven out of ten" person—you have created a much worse situation, in which you lost a couple of "nine out of ten" and "ten out of ten" people.

That is a risk you cannot afford, so you have to do the difficult thing and terminate the person you were wavering about. If you're still not sure, then ask yourself how often this person is coming up in conversations around the business, with other employees and clients. If you are hearing their name more than a few times a week and it's not to praise their work, then that is a sign you have a problem. People who don't quite fit have a habit of dominating conversations in HR and management meetings. These are the cases where you need to make an honest assessment and often deliver bad news.

It's worth saying that, occasionally, the problem is not the person but the role. A few times, I have moved someone in the seven and eight camp to another department or position and seen them transform into a nine or ten. But the norm is that someone who starts as a seven in your business is going to stay there. The longer you hold off making the decision to fire them, the harder it will be for all concerned.

No one likes being fired or having to fire people, but there are times when it simply cannot be avoided. As difficult as it may be for the person who is being asked to leave, it is the right thing for the business as a whole. And often it will be the right thing for that person, as disappointed and upset as they may be. For whatever combination of reasons, this role wasn't working out for them: they were struggling to make sales, build client relationships, or deliver work at the standard you expected. This is not the right environment for them to thrive. That is a stressful situation for anyone to be in, and you need to have empathy with how they feel and the reasons they may be failing. But unless there is a very clear path to rectifying those issues, then you have to act.

Once you are having the dreaded conversation, be both as clear and compassionate as possible. The news will probably not be a surprise since the person has very likely been warned already about their performance and possibly placed on an improvement plan. But it will still come as a shock. Make it clear that the decision has been taken and cannot be reversed, but also ask what you can do to help. Offer to stay in touch, to put them in contact with potential employers, and to help them with their job search. Once the conversation is over, make arrangements for them to leave as quickly as possible. Tell the rest of your team what has happened and give them the chance to ask questions.

None of this is pleasant for anyone involved. In the end, people mostly get fired because of a mistaken decision to recruit in the first place. In retrospect, it's easy to see that you hired the wrong person, they took the wrong job, and it was always destined to end like this. Unwinding these mistakes is still difficult. But it cannot be avoided. And it is far less painful if you act quickly and decisively, as soon as you have the necessary information and have taken the required steps.

People often don't talk about firing, because we tend to avoid difficult subjects. It's a lot more palatable to share your method for hiring people and making their dreams come true than how you go about getting rid of the people who are holding your business back. But these are two halves of the same coin. Hire enough people and you will end up firing some of them. If you accept that and learn how to do it properly, then you will save a lot of agony for yourself, your business, and even the people you decide to let go.

How to build a community

When I first started putting out content on social media about how to start a business, I never thought about building a community. I certainly didn't expect that, a few years later, I would be engaging with an audience of over 5 million across different channels, and running a business that exists to enable a massive community of people to help each other achieve their dreams.

What I have learned in that time is that community is a superpower for business: an incredible asset if you can nurture and harness it. When I say "community," I mean something that goes beyond a customer base. A community is something more dynamic, engaged, and passionate. This is about the people who don't just want to buy a pair of shoes from you, but who will collect every line you produce; who don't just play your video game but create content around it; who don't just buy your cookbooks but post about each of the recipes they have created from it.

Those are fans, and out of fans talking to each other, sharing their passion for what you do and making it a part of their lives, you build a community of people with a shared interest in your brand, its purpose, and the dream that powers it. That might be a literal community, like people who connect online to play *FIFA* or who come together in Peloton spin classes. Or it might be people who identify with your brand as part of their lifestyle—a cheeky Nando's and the latest drop from Adidas. In either case, it is at this point where passions, fandom, and consumption meet that you create a community.

This has always existed, but in a digitally connected world it is a more powerful force than ever. When you have a community, you are no longer just selling a product but helping to provide a lifestyle experience to people who give each other tips, compare achievements, share photos, and support each other. Your brand becomes a platform for people with the same interests to find each other and share their enjoyment of a particular hobby, experience, or lifestyle.

The importance of community is something that gives small businesses an advantage over big ones. Large companies in heavily regulated industries like finance may have huge customer bases, but they are also terrified of what happens when they communicate with them. What if people start asking them for things they can't do? In many cases, the corporate response is to try to minimize community rather than harness it. They think the risk outweighs the reward. That's a huge opportunity for smaller and more nimble brands, led by entrepreneurs who understand how to turn their customers into a community. It's why, sticking to finance, the big traditional companies can never replicate the kind of brand loyalty and engagement that challenger banks have earned.

With HelpBnk, the community is the most important thing we have by far. I can only help ten million people to achieve their dreams if most of the work is done by other people: the ones who give their time to answer people's questions, to give advice, and make connections on our platform. Those people do this because they believe in our purpose and the dream of a world that runs on the principle of #GiveWithoutTake. They give to the community because they enjoy it, and over time that helps it to grow and become stronger. They show up, online and sometimes in person, to support people who have asked for help to achieve their dream.

Can you build a community like that on purpose? The answer is yes and no. You can't force something that doesn't want to exist into being, but you can cultivate the early signs of it. In HelpBnk's case, we built a platform so that people would have a place to go and seek help: the basis of our community. In parallel, I have also put a huge amount of time into celebrating the people who give help and those who are achieving their dreams—showing the results of our work and stoking a sense of collective achievement. I make myself available to the community on social media as much as possible. I do giveaways and competitions. I do all this for free, or in the rare case that I ask for money—like the cost of buying this book—then I use all the proceeds to help fund more people's dreams.

In other words, I *invest* in the community. A bit like gardening, you don't know exactly what is going to grow and how well, but you need to do the right things to give it a chance. That might mean thinking about what you can do for your most loyal customers to turn them into passionate fans—for example a giveaway, a brand partnership, or early access to something new you are trying. It might involve events that bring together your customers and partners. Or it might mean working harder at your presence and content on social media to make it easier for people to engage with you and each other.

As you build a community, there is one thing to bear in mind. All these people probably have a lot in common, but that does not mean they have to agree about everything. And they certainly don't have to agree with you. I think almost everyone who is part of the HelpBnk community believes in helping people to achieve their dreams. Many probably agree with my opinion that our education system is broken and holding people back. But I know for a fact that plenty disagree with my cynical view towards property ownership: quite a lot of the people who are active on HelpBnk are trying to build their businesses in real estate or already have done. That is a good thing: a broad church is a strong one, and if you want everyone to agree about everything, then it's no longer a community but a cult.

You also have to beware obvious community killers— actions that will kill trust, loyalty, and engagement stone dead. It's fairly self-evident that if you lie to your community or try to exploit it (for example with unexpected price increases or service reductions) then people will turn on you. Almost as bad is to take the community for granted, or to underestimate its importance. In extreme cases, this can end up with a founder being at war with their community for ownership of the brand.

This is what happened with Beanie Babies, the stuffed toys that became a global craze around the turn of the millennium. It was a business that relied completely on the engagement of its fans and community: trading the toys, holding conventions, and trying to hunt down rare examples.

One of the biggest fans, Mary Beth Sobolewski, started

editing a magazine about Beanie Babies, which at its peak had a circulation of over a million readers. Her profile in the community got bigger and bigger until the owner of the manufacturer ended up suing both her and the publisher for breach of copyright. It was an example of when a brand tries to exercise too much control over the community that made it strong, not understanding that the two rely on each other. The community began to fragment, interest waned, and before long Beanie Babies were just another toy.

Community can be a powerful and volatile thing—one that's neither the sole creation of a business nor something it can entirely control. You have to respect your community, support it, and ultimately acknowledge that it is to some degree independent and must remain so. If you want to harness the power of a community to help drive your brand and support your dream, then you have to accept everything that comes with it.

That is the reality of bringing anyone into your business in whatever capacity. When you first have a business idea, it only exists in your head. Everything can be exactly as you imagined it and no one else can touch it. But soon you will have a cofounder, employees, customers, perhaps investors, and partners. Many more people are going to be a part of your business and helping to shape its destiny. You are going to have to share your dream and invite other people to help define it. If you accept that, and you want to involve the people who you need to grow the business and pursue the dream, then you also have to accept that more people means less personal control. You'll have to give up equity, delegate decisions, and, over time, let more and more other people steer the ship on your behalf.

That might feel like you are making your position weaker,

but in fact you are making your business stronger. You are building a bigger, better, and more durable vehicle. And once you have done so, and you are racing ever closer to your dream, I guarantee you won't care who is sitting in the driver's seat.

This has been the longest chapter of the book, which is appropriate because there is no more important subject in business than people. Even in a world where AI is playing a growing role, and many traditional jobs will cease to exist, it will remain true that you cannot build a brilliant business or fulfill an ambitious dream without great people around you. But those people also need to be given the right direction and leadership. Your business will not grow and your dream will not advance simply by accumulating a team and continuing to do things the same way as you always have. Real growth, at every stage of a business journey, comes through risk taking. It's risk that delivers the real rewards, allows you to constantly reinvent your business, and to make progress towards your dream. It's risk, more than anything else, that allows you to get lucky.

II

Develop a Risk Muscle

It's time for a confession. Everything you have been reading so far, all the advice, the experiences, the anecdotes—all of it is coming from a known criminal. A self-confessed lawbreaker. A crime I committed and then posted about on social media. Before they come to slap on the cuffs, let me explain.

In my defense, I broke the law for good reason—to try to help people. It was not long after we had launched HelpBnk, and like most start-ups we wanted people to know we existed. We needed attention. We needed to advertise.

The problem with advertising is that everyone is trying to do it. Your advert goes in a magazine, on the side of a bus, in Google's search results, or onto someone's LinkedIn feed along with countless others. People learn to filter this stuff out. Our eyes slide past the wallpaper of billboards and promoted posts.

That's why having an advert on its own is almost never enough. You also need to do something that reinforces the message—something unusual, memorable, or different. For us at HelpBnk, the message was that we wanted to help people for free. And the something—the stunt—was that we would get our advertising space for free as well. One free thing to support another.

So we printed a load of those little poster ads you see on subway cars with our logo and the words "We didn't pay for this advert so you don't have to pay for help." Rather than calling up a media company to get them placed, we just went on the London Underground for an hour and I started sticking them up inside the subway cars where there were empty ad boards. We put some of the money it would have cost to buy the space into envelopes and started giving it out to people traveling in those same cars.

Now, you might be thinking: that's a bit rich. If he's so successful, why doesn't he just pay for the ads? Why risk getting caught breaking the law just to save a little bit of money? And why did he feel entitled to do that in the first place?

All those questions went through my head too. I wondered if it was ethical, but as I went around on the Tube, I kept noticing all these empty spaces where ads were meant to be. We wouldn't be taking space that someone else had paid for.

As for being able to afford to pay, doing so would almost have defeated the point of the campaign. If I had bought the ads and had them placed through the official channels, no one would have noticed. But by taking the space, breaking the law, and creating content around it, we were able to attract eyeballs online. Ironically, the ads were worth more to us because we didn't pay for them. The story of how we'd placed our ads became much more important than the words on them. It wasn't about saving a bit of money but drastically increasing our chances of getting noticed.

All that being said, it was a risk. What I was doing is called billposting and it's a criminal offense. By filming everything, I was making it even worse, because that is not permitted on London Underground without their prior permission. As my team and I carried our equipment into London Bridge station to get started, a message blared over the loud speakers to this effect. When I asked a station staff member what would happen if I filmed anyway, they said the British Transport Police would be called.

I went ahead because sometimes you have to **break the rules to be successful**. In certain circumstances, you have to take a risk in order to achieve your objective. I knew that the only chance of getting *any* traction with our ad campaign was to do something that reinforced the message of giving away our help for free. That meant taking the space without paying so that we could give lots of people help for nothing. In my eyes, it was a risk that paid off. No one has (yet) pursued me as a result. Perhaps I'm taking another risk by drawing attention to it here.

I'm telling you this not because I want everyone to go on billposting sprees around the country—and whatever you do, please don't break the law. The reason is that I need you to understand the importance of risk. As you build your business and move towards your dream, you will be confronted with many decision points and crossroads moments. Do you take on a customer who is too big for your current operation to handle (and figure out how to scale up as you go)? Do you accept an offer to expand your business into a new location? Do you diversify the range of products or services you are selling? Do you hire great people when you can find them, or wait for customers to come on board before growing your headcount? Do you do something that could get you noticed but might also get you into trouble?

The running of any business is a constant exercise in understanding and weighing up risk. There are risks you should take and others it would be better to swerve. But I can promise you that **unless you learn to take good risks, your business will not succeed and your dream will fade away**. There is simply no success that comes without the consistent ability to pursue the right risks at the right time, ensuring that enough of them will pay off.

It's back to the idea I debunked at the very beginning of the book: "the harder I work, the luckier I get." Most entrepreneurs will tell you that the true version of that statement is: "the more risks I take, the luckier I get." Risk will be needed at every stage of the journey towards your dream. Some will succeed, others will fail, but you have to keep taking risks and improving your judgment about where and how to take them.

That is the key thing: not taking risks indiscriminately, but taking them well. Risk is a poorly understood topic and many people have the wrong ideas about it. They think that if you say take a risk, it means jumping off a cliff and hoping for the best. The opposite is true. Being a risk-taker doesn't mean putting on a blindfold and stumbling about. It doesn't mean crossing your fingers and hoping that every gamble pays off. It's actually about being smart, calculated, and precise. About knowing when to try something and how to stack the odds in your favor. You can be a good risk-taker, and you become a better one the more you do it. In this chapter, I'll explain how this works: why risk is a muscle, how you can build it, and the importance of exercising it regularly.

Imagine best- AND worst-case scenarios

My basic thesis about risk is very simple: accept that you could lose everything, but mitigate the chance that you will.

This is the start of becoming a good risk-taker. Before you can think about what you stand to gain, you have to understand what you have to lose. Imagine the worst-case scenario for a minute. Put yourself there and ask yourself how bad it would really be if this all goes belly-up. What would you lose and how would you react?

This is the calculation most people go through when starting a business. A classic example was Natasha, aka the Vegan Patty Lady. When she rang our doorbell, she had a dream but hadn't fully committed to it. It was a tasty dream with all the right ingredients: she wanted to own the market in making Jamaican patties with a vegan filling. This was a big idea that had a purpose rooted in personal pain. Having suffered with serious asthma throughout her life, Tasha had noticed her symptoms improved dramatically when she turned to a vegan diet. Now she wanted to promote that lifestyle to more people, by showing that a food people love can be just as brilliant when it's vegan, and far better for you.

But she wasn't sure. It wasn't the first time she had tried to launch a business. In fact, she had a few failures behind her already. She and her husband, Adonye, had been saving up money to buy a house. Now they faced a choice: fund the dream business or keep saving until they could afford to get the house?

Many entrepreneurs stand on this precipice before getting started. Launching their business will mean quitting their well-paying job, using up savings, even getting a new mortgage on the house to unlock some funding. Will they do it? Will they risk it?

You already know my answer to that question (don't buy the bloody house!). But at this critical moment, I don't matter. Only you, your family, and loved ones do. It's your decision. Your risk. And that is why you have to take yourself to the worst-case scenario. What would it be like and what would your next step be? If that is going to be an intolerable situation for you, then it may not be the right risk (or the right time for you to take that risk). Perhaps you need to spend a bit more time building up a fighting fund, or getting a partner on board. Our appetite for risk is purely individual and it changes over time. You have to know your willingness to take this particular risk at this moment in time. Visualizing the worst-case scenario is an important part of working that out.

And if you think that you *can* stomach that scenario, then what is there to lose? In your head you've been through that already. It won't be nice, but you know what you would do. You could live with that failure. At this point, you have to flip your mindset around and start inspiring yourself with the *best*-case scenario. Turn that nightmare into a dream. Allow yourself to taste a little bit of your future success.

That is how it was for Natasha. I knew that she and Adonye had already thought a lot about what would happen if their savings were swallowed by another failed venture. So after she rang the doorbell, I mobilized the HelpBnk community to give them a boost. I organized for 150 people to gather at the staircase and set her a challenge. We would do a tasting, but with a twist. I wanted Tasha to bake the world's biggest vegan patty, which we would then serve to the invited guests. We would break a world record and gather feedback about the product at the same time—marketing and market research in one go.

Despite a few mishaps along the way, including an emergency stop in the van that put the record-breaking pastry in peril, Tasha and her patty made it to Twickenham. The waiting crowd cheered her on and devoured the brilliant product with its walnut and mushroom filling. It couldn't have been clearer that she had a potential winner on her hands. But there was still one problem. Did the couple want to put their hard-earned savings into this dream? There was no question that Tasha had the passion and she had the product. But it had all gone wrong before. Would it be different this time? Would they decide to take the risk?

It was Adonye who summed it up. Yes, they had been saving for a long time for that house, but putting some of that money into the business could be a case of one step back to take ten steps forward. Getting the business off the ground would generate money that could buy a house later.

This was a great example of how to really think through and understand a risk. Natasha and Adonye were putting their savings on the line, but in a way that could deliver a significant financial upside over time. What's more, not doing so would have meant Tasha putting her dream on the shelf, probably forever. The best-case scenario was that they could have it all: the business she was desperate to run *and* the house they'd been saving for. And in the worst-case scenario? In Adonye's words: "It's only money. If it takes five grand for my wife to follow her dream, then that's life."

We did a deal: they put $6,500 into the Vegan Patty Lady business and I matched it. Tasha had her funding. Since then, she has sold thousands of patties, got the product stocked by half a dozen retailers, and funded equipment purchases through crowdfunding. All because she took a risk that was carefully considered, taking into account both best- and worst-case scenarios. Natasha knew that she was betting on her passion and her dream. She had a purpose to guide and propel her. And she and Adonye knew that life would go on if the investment never realized a return. It was only money.

Perhaps most importantly, they knew that failing to chase this dream was not really an option at all. They broke down their risk, looked at it from all angles, and eventually decided that there was only one choice to make.

That is why you have to think through the different out-comes before you make a big decision and take what feels like a risk. Once you have done that and allowed yourself to live with the potential consequences, the fear can't hurt you any-more. You will be going down either one road or the other. You can cope with the outcome. You're ready to take the risk.

Build the muscle

However you do it, you are taking a risk to start a business. So many things can go wrong: a stronger competitor may emerge, the economy may go down the tubes, your warehouse might burn down, a partner might run away with your profits, em-ployees might desert you. Even a small business is a complex ecosystem dependent on many different things working to-gether. If just one goes badly wrong, it can all fall to pieces.

Every entrepreneur, however experienced or well-funded, faces the threat of collapse and the risk of failure. You might lose your business and all the money that was invested in it. You take that risk because it's the only way to pursue your dream.

But you can't just sit on that one risk and get comfortable. Remember that this journey is about lots of small steps, all tak-ing you a little bit closer to the dream. You can't get there in one big hop, and a single bold gambit isn't going to be enough. To make the business successful, you are going to have to keep on taking risks. Risk is how you started a business, and risk is how you will grow it. The really dangerous risk as an entrepre-neur is to assume that what you have been doing will keep on working and that nothing needs to change.

That's why I talk about risk as a muscle you have to build up

over time. Sizing up risks is a skill you can develop with practice. And like any muscle, it gets stronger the more you train
and use it. You get good at taking risks by taking risks. You
build confidence with the ones that pay off and learn from
those that don't. In the process, you realize that a lot of what
we call risk is simply a product of fear. In fact those risks are
just choices: once you've learned to think of them as normal
business decisions with pros and cons, you will stop being
afraid of them. You can see the odds more clearly.

In your business journey, some risks will be of your own
making and others will be presented to you as choices. One
week you might be thinking about the possibility of expanding
into a new territory or launching a new product line. And the
next, a customer might approach you and ask if you can do
something that you don't currently. Or can you rapidly scale
up the service you are offering them, and perhaps give them a
dedicated team?

Those are opportunities but also risks. They may take you
into unfamiliar territory, require you to hire more quickly than
you are comfortable with, or to stretch yourself and your key
people more thinly. In deciding whether or not to press ahead,
apply the same tests as you did when starting the business in
the first place. Remember, if you followed my steps, then that
business grew out of something you liked or were good at
doing. It's helping you to fulfill a purpose and move towards a
dream. When it comes to judging risks, ask yourself: are those
things also true of this new venture or brand extension? Is it
aligned with the purpose? Will it take you a step closer to the
dream? Will it be fun?

Looking back, I know I could have avoided a lot of bad
decisions by knowing my purpose more clearly and applying those tests. It would have saved me from going into

partnerships that ended badly or embarking on side ventures that proved to be dead ends. **The best way to ensure you take the right risks as you build your business is to remember why you started it in the first place.** Over time, you will get better at working out quickly what is going to help you fulfill your purpose and what is going to get in the way. You will develop an instinct because you have done the work to build the risk muscle (I once heard someone say that instinct is just passion in disguise, which is a great description).

Deciding *what* risks to take is one big part of the equation, and another is deciding *how* to take them. If you are smart, you can make a bold move in a relatively safe way. Take Bizzies, a sweet business I launched to promote the idea of #GiveWithoutTake. That's a confectionery brand with a simple message and a clear purpose: a sweet that can make dreams come true. Buy it, and the profit we make will go back into supporting people with their dreams.

It was a simple idea, but also a risky one. Because although I've run a lot of businesses, I've never been near the confectionery industry. And it just happens to be one of the most competitive, saturated markets in the world. Global giants battle it out for the money you spend on your next sugar high. It's a brutal, cut-throat business and a tiny player like me shouldn't stand a chance.

If, for example, I had decided to sink my entire fortune into building Bizzies on the basis that this was a complicated industry that required a significant level of investment to break into, it would have been a huge risk. I would have been betting the farm in an area where I have no knowledge, experience, or network. It would have meant having to learn about all sorts of things I didn't want to learn about, like how the products are manufactured, packaged, and distributed. It would have been difficult, we probably would have failed, and my life would have been taken over by trying to beat Mars and Nestlé rather than trying to help people with their dreams.

I didn't do any of that. Instead, I found a partner, a confectionery start-up called Tasty Mates, which makes vegan treats with all-natural ingredients. We launched a single line—a sour passionfruit gummy called the Passionate One—under the Bizzies brand. And we co-ventured: I got access to their expertise in manufacturing and distributing the product, and they got my support in promoting their brand along with the one we created together. In the process, I was able to do something I really wanted to do—to launch a sweet brand aligned with HelpBnk's purpose—without the risk of having to create that business from scratch.

This is what I mean by building the risk muscle. Part of it is developing an appetite to take risk in the first place, accepting that you will stagnate if you stand still. Another part is learning to judge risk and test each big decision against your anchors of purpose and the dream. And the final part is being clever about how you approach your next bold move. Can you pursue the opportunity you have spotted in a derisked way—in other words, can you take a smarter risk? Should you run it as a partnership, pilot program, or initial promotion? That is how to be nimble and flexible about risk. Remember: the key is to **accept that you could lose everything, but to mitigate the chances that you will**. You should never take a risk where you haven't thought about the worst-case scenario or taken some precautions to try to avoid it. Being a smart risk-taker and learning to derisk your decisions is as important as the willingness to be bold in the first place.

Know when to stand your ground

The early hours of the morning are not perhaps the best time to take your next risk, but on this occasion I did. It was around 3 a.m., in the relatively early days of Fluid, and I had finally found time to research an idea that had been rattling around my head. Anyone who has lived in Hong Kong knows what a big deal the annual Rugby Sevens tournament is. People come from all over the world to watch and take part. But all the focus was on what was happening inside the stadium, and many businesses suffered a loss of footfall as a result. What if we did something for them? My idea was simple: an online portal that would promote everything else going on in Hong Kong during the event that wasn't rugby. If it went well and we attracted an audience, there might be a revenue model in getting local businesses to advertise on our website. At best, I'd have created a meaningful side business that could be used to promote the Fluid brand to potential clients. And at worst, I'd have made my point about the rugby.

It was while I was researching the idea in the small hours that I stumbled across something that suddenly made it seem a lot more interesting. A URL: www.hksevens.com. Surely this was a mistake: the tournament organizers must have locked this down? But they hadn't. Their website was www.hksevens.com.hk. They had somehow neglected to purchase the dot-com address for their own website. It was sitting there available for just $15. I bought it on the spot.

Initially, I hoped that I might be able to partner up with the organizers. We had a meeting and I offered to work with them, but they made it clear they weren't interested. Then I faced a decision. In the cold light of day, holding the URL very similar to the official one started to feel like a risk. I knew I hadn't done anything wrong: I wasn't trying to imitate them, sell tickets or get money off them by making them buy it back. I just wanted to run my little side hustle and see how it went. Still, in the back of my mind, I started to have doubts.

That was the summer and the tournament happens in spring. Tickets go on sale in December. When that window opened, suddenly we had a massive traffic spike to our website. Our comment board filled up with questions about how to get hold of tickets. And soon a cease and desist letter arrived from lawyers on behalf of Hong Kong Sevens, telling us to stop infringing on their trademark. This wasn't some friendly approach asking us nicely. It was an aggressive lawyer's letter, threatening to sue Fluid for loss of income and to make Helen and me personally liable.

At this point, there was every reason to fold my hand and meekly comply. The website wasn't important or a core part of our business. It had been a stray idea that met a random opportunity. I could give in to the threat and the whole thing would not have cost me much more than the initial $15.

But I don't really like being told to stop when I'm almost certain I have done nothing wrong. So, rather than shutting down the website, I hired some fancy lawyers of my own. And in the legal back-and-forth, it emerged that Hong Kong Sevens didn't actually (at that time) own the trademark they had accused us of infringing. It's illegal to claim you own a trademark when you don't. Checkmate. A settlement followed, which involved them paying us money to obtain the URL rather than the other way around.

This was an example of where risk can happen to you, rather than you deciding to commit to it. Perhaps I'd taken a small risk in deciding to press ahead with the website, but the real risk was deciding not to comply with the threatening demand from a Magic Circle legal firm. At that point, I was risking serious consequences by doubling down.

So why did I take this risk, and why am I making a point of telling you this story? I think it illustrates an experience many of you will have as entrepreneurs. There will come a time when someone comes knocking on your door with a warning or threat of some kind. This might be friendly, from a friend or investor worried that you are doing the wrong thing. Or it may come from a competitor who is warning you to get the hell off their lawn. This is the final part of the risk muscle: knowing when and how to hold your ground.

This is a balancing act, because you should always be open to feedback and advice, but you should never be easily swayed from an idea to which you are committed. If you've already put that idea through the tests we discussed above, knowing that it aligns with your purpose and will help to further your dream, then it should take something very compelling to change your mind: a new piece of information, involving some serious complication of which you were previously unaware.

The thing about risk is that other people will often try to dissuade you from it. You can't let their fears cloud your judgment. Always remember that if you don't learn to take risks, you are agreeing to live your life according to other people's rules and priorities. Diverge from them, and I can guarantee at least some people will try to stop you. You have to learn when to block out those voices, and stop them from eroding your conviction.

If, after all that, you are still unsure about taking a risk, then you can apply the final test: what are you doing it for? If you're taking a risk in order to build something and move towards your dream, then there is every chance you are doing the right thing. Even if the bet doesn't pay off, you will learn something through the failure. Back yourself unless you can see an exceptionally good reason not to.

The less healthy type of risk is one that offers you some kind of dodge or shortcut. The opportunity to cut a corner in a way that instinct tells you may be a problem. This is where you need to be wary of risk and highly discriminate in your approach.

I learned this at an early stage with Fluid. I'd hired an accountant who had come recommended, and who advised me that we should engage in a practice called carrying forward income, so that it was taxed in the next financial year rather than the current one. She told me it was entirely legal and that it made financial sense. This was in 2003, when the Hong Kong economy was still suffering from the SARS outbreak, and the idea of reducing that year's tax bill was appealing. I said yes, even though I felt uneasy about a financial practice that I didn't fully understand and that sounded too good to be true.

Fast forward three years and we had a new accountant, who quickly informed me that we had in fact broken the rules and escaped tax that ought to have been paid. He worked with the Hong Kong tax authorities to reach a settlement that amounted to a backdated tax demand without additional fines—probably a kinder outcome than we deserved. And I vowed that I would never dabble in creative accounting again.

In the process, I had learned that this is the worst kind of risk to take: I hadn't fully done my research, I trusted someone simply because they told me what I wanted to hear, and I was trying to get something for nothing. Ever since, I have always tried to avoid risks that were about schemes and shortcuts, and to focus on those where I am doing something that has the chance to build sustainable value for one of my businesses.

Those are risks you never have to feel queasy about, even when they go wrong.

The risk muscle is one of the most important skills you can develop as a business owner. I call it a muscle because we all have it, and we can all build it with the right sort of training. It's hard steeling yourself to take risks in a world that often tells you not to, but this is a nonnegotiable part of the journey we are on. Your dream is not going to fall into your lap and you are going to have to take risks to achieve it. But if you follow the steps I have set out, then you will learn that risk is not something to be feared but simply part of the job. (You'll also learn that it can be a lot of fun.)

Risk is one of the most important muscles you will need as an entrepreneur, but it's not the only one. To win over the long term, you will also need something else that everyone can have but too many people don't. Our next subject is one of the most simple and obvious in this book, but it's also one of the most important. It's an idea that's incredibly easy to understand, and much harder to implement. Probably more than anything, this makes the difference between the people who dream dreams and the ones who achieve them. I am talking about persistence.

12.

Keep Going

When you think of business role models, the people that come to mind didn't usually live 500 years ago and did their best work with sharp objects. But an unlikely inspiration of mine is the Renaissance artist Michelangelo, and specifically his most famous creation—the statue of David preparing for his epic battle against Goliath, which has stood seventeen feet high since he completed it in 1504, and is generally regarded as the most important sculpture ever made.

Now, I am not an artist, an art lover, or someone remotely qualified to tell you about why this is such a legendary work. I can't remember the last time I picked up a paintbrush, and we would all be in trouble if I tried to carve anything with a chisel. But ever since I learned the story of how Michelangelo made *David*, I have thought that it is one of the best illustrations there is of how success is achieved.

Because this artwork has stood the test of time and so has the name of its sculptor, you might assume that *David* had always been destined for greatness.

The real story is both different and more interesting. When Michelangelo first put chisel to stone in 1501, the idea for this statue had been around for much longer than he had been alive. He was twenty-six years old, and the sculpture had first been broached as far back as 1408. A different sculptor first began working on it in 1464, and another one had a go in 1476, the year after Michelangelo was born. Both gave up, deeming the gigantic slab of marble from which *David* would eventually be hewn to be of insufficient quality. The greatest sculpture in the world was hiding in that stone, but those craftsmen couldn't find it.

For a quarter of a century, this hunk of rock sat and waited—too expensive to discard, but apparently too imperfect to sculpt. And then came Michelangelo. For three years he tackled the work in his own painstaking way: hidden away, refusing to let anyone see it, eating little, and sleeping in his clothes.

I sometimes wonder if, during those long days locked away in the dark with his masterpiece, Michelangelo knew he was creating something so special. Could he have guessed that people would still be admiring and discussing his sculpture half a millennium later? We'll never know. But what we *do* know is how absurd this would have sounded to anyone else—frankly how unlikely it sounds to us even now, knowing how things turned out.

That is why I love the story of how Michelangelo made *David* almost as much as I admire the work itself. It's a brilliant and beautiful example of how things can turn out differently to what most people expect. How what people call common sense can be so badly mistaken. Of how extraordinary things can happen when people believe in their purpose *and* carry it through to the very end.

The reason I tell you about Michelangelo isn't to try to draw some lofty lesson from his sculpture or to try to make myself look culturally sophisticated. It's because it shows us something very simple and relatable: even for one of the greatest geniuses who ever lived, talent wasn't enough. What made the difference was his willingness to carry on. To keep on working for three years without much sleep or food, locked away in a dark room, working on a task that more experienced sculptors had deemed impossible. To persist.

Probably none of us are able to do what he did in artistic terms. But we are *all* capable of emulating the basic ability that allowed him to create *David*. We can all be determined. We can all keep going. We can all learn to screen out the naysayers with their warnings and "common sense." That is persistence, one of the most important human skills, one of the simplest and sadly one of the most lacking. Anyone can harness it, but far too many people don't, or haven't fully grasped its meaning.

That's why this next part is dedicated to dedication: how to carry on even when the odds seem stacked against us and it would be so much easier to hold up our hands. This is the easy bit that's paradoxically also the really hard bit. Far too many people give up, at the wrong time and for the wrong reasons. In this chapter, I'll show how you can avoid their fate, learn persistence, and keep your dream alive until it's finally within reach.

Pure persistence

I still remember one of the very first things I did after Helen and I set up Fluid. I sat down and wrote a list. On it were fifty names: all the big, flashy brands active in Hong Kong that I wanted us to work for. It was my bucket list of dream clients. For a completely new agency with no track record, it was an almost ludicrously high bar to set.

In our first month of trading, I contacted every single name. Most did not even reply and not a single one agreed to a meeting. It was a bad start, and I might have decided then that I had been too ambitious. But I didn't tear up my list. I kept on contacting those companies, and when I couldn't get an answer from one person, I would try another. When someone did engage with me, I would keep up the contact, whether through sending them a seasonal greeting, an article they might like to read, or thoughts on some aspect of their business that related to our work.

The purpose of this was to stay visible and to remain front-of-mind. The worst thing you can be in any business is forgotten. By contrast, if you have remained available, then you will be top of someone's list when the moment arrives that they actively want to buy whatever it is you're selling. My approach was also about adding value: not pestering the same people with the same offer week after week, but giving them something a little different, a little useful, and asking for nothing in return. If you keep doing that, then you give yourself the best chance of turning a no into a yes.

That's how it was at Fluid. Within the first year, I had several names on that list as clients. After nine years, we had worked with *every single one of them*. Some developed into long-term relationships and others were fairly small projects, but all of them went from never having heard of Fluid to choosing to work with us. That only happened through persistence. By prising open the doors of one or two household brands, we were able to attract others. Our profile grew and our brand became established. It helped that the work was good, of course, but the product or service on its own is never enough. You have to sell it to succeed, and to sell you simply have to be persistent.

That is a lesson that anyone who sells something for a living learns quickly. You cannot succeed if you are willing to take no for an answer, or accept easily that someone is ignoring you.

The best salespeople don't give up just because someone has rejected their pitch. When they think there is still an opportunity, perhaps at a later date or with a slightly different offer, they will keep going until they have found the right moment and the right pitch to get that person to say yes.

As someone who has essentially worked in sales for thirty years, and has hired and fired endless sales reps, I know that the difference between the people who do and don't deliver is persistence. Mediocre salespeople follow up a handful of times and then give up unless the door opens for them. Whereas real closers find a way to keep the conversation and engagement going. They don't bombard their target with endless, unsolicited messages that are likely to annoy them. Instead, they try to stay relevant, remind the potential client that they exist, and form some kind of relationship, however fleeting. They persist with lots of things that aren't a sales pitch, until the moment arrives when they can sell to that person. Put simply, they stay in the game, and that gives them the chance to win it. Most businesses are on some level a persistence game: you have to survive for long enough to give yourself the chance to make the life-changing deal. And survival only comes if you grit your teeth and decide to keep going.

Why is it persistence, something so simple, that separates the winners and losers? It might sound like an unsatisfying answer: surely the dividing line is more to do with skill, personality, or experience. I can promise you it's not. If I had the choice between hiring a skillful person or a persistent one, I'd choose the second every time, for a very simple reason: if you are persistent, it allows you to get lucky. If you carry on for long enough, and give yourself enough chances to make the sale, and stay available to the right people, then something is going to fall your way. One of the people you've been persisting with is going to need what you were selling. The persistent person is going to achieve something that the skillful one told you wasn't possible, simply because they gave themselves more chances to get lucky.

People talk about being lucky and unlucky in business as if these are completely freak events outside of their control. The truth is that you can hack luck and stack the odds in your favor, but only if you persist. If you keep giving yourself a chance, then the world is going to reward you with more opportunities. What we call luck and put down to chance or higher powers is often just boring maths. You were more visible to more people requiring your product or service, so you got "luckier" than the other person who gave up on the people who stopped talking to him. In that situation, your real fortune is that not everyone else who is competing in your field tried as hard as you. They didn't carry on as long and they weren't motivated by the same sense of purpose.

Persistence is an edge in business, and in life, because most people don't show it (hence why I will always hire the persistent person, on the basis that I can teach them the skill part). If you are persistent in how you run your business and pursue your dream, it will set you apart from most people who are trying to do the same thing. Before long, you will have become the luckiest person you know.

Persistence through adversity

At the time of writing, there are nine companies in the world that are worth more than a trillion dollars. Seven of them are based in the United States. And two of them once very nearly went bankrupt, within a year of each other.

The better-known case is Apple, around a decade before it changed the world (and its own fortunes) by introducing the iPhone. A succession of product launches had failed, its iconic founder Steve Jobs was still exiled from the company, and the company had been losing money for twelve consecutive years. In 1997, it lost a billion dollars, which is what it makes today in the time it takes for Tim Cook to scratch his nose, but back then was more than a third of the company's entire market capitalization. To put it in technical terms, they were going bust.

What happened next has become a familiar story. Jobs returned, a partnership with Microsoft helped to save the company, and within a year Apple had delivered the first in a run of innovative product launches—the iMac—that would build the brand into the behemoth we know today.

The year before Jobs breathed life back into Apple, a fellow member of today's trillion-dollar club had also gone very close to the wall. This was Nvidia, relatively smaller in scope compared to the company that had helped to define the rise of the personal computer in the 1980s. Almost no one knew these guys. It would be a very long time before the company became a household name, synonymous with the AI boom.

Back in 1996, Nvidia was trying to get a foothold in the graphics processing market. It was developing chips for games consoles and decided to diverge from the standard model to get an edge—enabling game designers to work with four- rather than three-sided pixels. It didn't work. Software providers including Microsoft only wanted to support the standard template, and Nvidia's first launch was a disaster. It left the company short on money and knowing that the next product had to succeed to avoid bankruptcy. When it went live, Nvidia only had enough cash in the bank to pay its people for one more month. It had microchips to sell but wasn't entirely sure they were going to work. "It was fifty-fifty," founder Jensen Huang told *The New Yorker* in a 2023 interview about the prospects of the product being a success, "but we were going out of business anyway."[1] The gamble paid off. A million chips were sold in four months. A company had been saved, and a trillion-dollar success story had been born.

It's a great story, showing that even the most famous companies in the world once stared disaster in the face, and had to persist through adversity to succeed. Just as importantly, Jensen Huang didn't try to brush that near disaster under the carpet. He reveled in the memory of that adversity and made it core to his company's identity. He made the phrase "our company is thirty days from going out of business" a core part of his presentations and a regular rallying cry, even long after it had ceased to be literally true.

As the business grew and became more successful, he didn't want the people working in it to lose the sense of urgency that had defined it in its toughest moment. Persistence through adversity hadn't just saved the company in a tight spot; it would also be the trait that guaranteed its future.

Elsewhere, Huang has talked about his belief that adversity is one of the greatest teachers and how people who learn to persist through it are those who will succeed in life. "People with very high expectations have very low resilience. Unfortunately, resilience matters in success. I don't know how to teach it to you, except for I hope suffering happens to you."[2]

He said that to an audience of students at Stanford University and his message was that their intelligence, their great grades, and their networks were not going to be enough in life. They also had to cultivate the resilience that only comes through falling down and getting back up again. Through learning what it means to fail and find another way. Through being taught by life what it really means to be persistent. That has been the story of his life, and that is how he has built one of the most successful companies in the world. As he also said at the Stanford event: "To this day, I use the phrase pain and suffering inside our company with great glee . . . [I say] boy, this is going to cause a lot of pain and suffering. And I mean that in a happy way, because you want to train [and] you want to refine the character of your company . . . Character isn't formed out of smart people, it's formed out of people who suffered."

I have my own version of this phrase, which I sometimes say to motivate myself: if you stop, someone dies. That is the level of determination it takes to be successful when there is so much standing in your way. Unless you are truly persistent, you are eventually going to encounter a problem that feels too big to overcome. You are going to give up. It's during moments of real adversity that your persistence will be tested, and you will learn whether you actually understand the meaning of the word.

I have seen this happen countless times. People fail, fold up their tent, and then they tell the world a story. They say that the financial crisis happened, a pandemic happened, that an unstoppable and much richer competitor emerged, that Google or Meta changed its algorithm and killed their business model. They say it was inevitable and couldn't be helped. They say it was bad luck.

Sometimes they are right, but in most cases this is a false story told to make them feel better. They didn't have to fail and their business didn't have to go bust. There was another way if they had looked closely enough or pushed harder. It's not polite to say, but these people gave up. The kitchen got too hot and they left. They were asked to reinvent their business model, make drastic cuts to their workforce, or start doing something they thought was beneath them, and they decided they couldn't or wouldn't do it. They decided that persistence was too hard and giving up was preferable. They didn't persevere for long enough to get lucky, and blamed bad luck for their failure instead.

I put this in blunt terms because my experience of business is that it really can be that simple. When things get really hard, which they will, the single path on which your business has been traveling splits into two. You either give up or you go through hell to carry on. You face the choice of whether or not to persist.

It's not easy, and you're not guaranteed to succeed if you choose the second route. I still remember how sick I felt in 2007 when our biggest client, a major bank, rang us up to say that they were suspending payments to suppliers for ninety days. They owed us a seven-figure sum, which we had been relying on to make payroll. For weeks I felt ill, struggled to sleep, and thought every day about the business collapsing. I think a part of me *wanted* it to fail so that I would be off the hook. But we had also come so far, done so much, and I knew this was the business that would change my and Helen's lives if we could carry it through to completion. Enough of the fifteen-year-old who had nothing was still in me to stop me from giving up. So we kept going and, as I explained earlier, we survived through a combination of swimming against the tide and getting lucky that the market picked up before most people expected (a good example of how persisting for long enough gives you the chance of getting lucky). By the time our major client finally paid us, we'd already won other work and were no longer reliant on that money for survival.

The interesting thing is that if Fluid had failed in 2007, I know I would have blamed the one massive client that let us down. I'd have said that you can't account for not being paid the biggest bill you are owed. And I would have been wrong. It would have been a self-serving story that ignored the fact that I'd allowed us to become too reliant on a single client. And it would have been a false narrative, because the failure would not have been the result of bad luck or even just bad business planning, but a failure of persistence.

There are two points to understand here. The first is that adversity will happen to you and your business whatever you do, and it will require serious persistence to overcome. And the second is that if you do persist, your prize will be more than simple survival. You will also be molded by that experience and emerge stronger. As a result, you will not be surprised by the next dose of adversity—some unexpected cost, failure in your supply chain, customer nightmare, or act of God. You will be ready for it.

Persistence is needed to face the adversity that any business encounters, and **your persistence—both individually and collectively—increases through adversity**. It's another muscle that you can develop. That's why the ability to keep going is so important. It will get you through today's problem and make you stronger to face the next one. It will be the guarantee that your company is going to survive and grow.

Strange as it may sound, you will learn to enjoy these moments. That sick feeling in the pit of your stomach is a reminder that you made it through before, and you will make it through again. Your business will survive, if you really need it to. You will find a way. Your dream will persist.

Pivot to persist

When I bang on about the importance of persistence and the need to keep going, I need you to understand one important nuance. I'm worried you might be thinking that all this talk of persistence sounds suspiciously similar to the old cliché about hard work. But it's different.

By persistence, I don't mean that you should put your head down and keep walking in the same direction, no matter what happens. This is a game won not by the people who work the hardest, but those who work the smartest. By people whose persistence is driven by a purpose and directed by a dream. Persistence is about guts but it's also about brains—working out the route that gives you the best chance of survival and long-term success. Often that will be something different from what has taken you this far.

The real meaning of persistence is to carry on *and to evolve as you go*. Whatever kind of business you are running, the world is constantly changing around you and you must change with it. You can't assume that what has made you successful will continue to deliver the goods. You have to adapt and adjust. You have to be nimble. A critical part of persistence is learning when and how to *pivot*.

There's a reason that some of the most famous products in the world began life as one thing and became famous for another. The ubiquitous material we know as Bubble Wrap wasn't actually designed as packaging: its inventors were trying to create wallpaper, and then tried to use their product to insulate greenhouses. Only after a couple of years did they find the mainstream application, when IBM started using it to pack their massive mainframe computers before shipping them to customers.

Much later, in 2010, two entrepreneurs built an app called Burbn, which allowed you to record your location, make plans to meet up in a certain place with your friends, and share photos. It was complicated, unsuccessful, and I can almost guarantee that you have never heard of it.

The founders of Burbn soon realized that, while most of their users weren't engaging with the key features of the app, they *were* using the photo-sharing part. So they stripped back their plans, pivoted the business, and created a more straightforward photo app. They called it Instagram.

Those are just two examples of businesses that became successful because they persisted until they landed on the right business model. This is the story of many more famous brands than you would think: Starbucks originally sold coffee beans for you to brew at home, Netflix sent you DVDs in the post, YouTube was a dating service. If they had persisted in a dumb way, all of those household names would now have been long forgotten. But because they persisted through pivoting, working out the business model that most customers actually wanted, they have become some of the most successful brands in the world.

This kind of persistence may be needed early in the life of a business, when it is still trying to figure out its approach. Or it could come at a point when the business model has been established but is walloped by some kind of freak event. That happened to us at Fluid in 2003 when the SARS pandemic struck East Asia. This was the kind of airborne virus with which the world became grimly familiar in 2020, and for six months it had the same effect on society. In Hong Kong, as was the case across much of the region, life temporarily shut down. With it, much of our business disappeared overnight. A large part of our income had been branding work, and suddenly businesses weren't being launched, campaigns weren't being run, and marketing promotions weren't needed.

If you'd told me at the beginning of that year that we would effectively be shutting down our branding business in a short space of time, I would have had a meltdown. But in the event, there were opportunities to pivot. As would happen on a different scale during Covid, the pandemic accelerated the shift to doing business online. Consumer-facing brands were starting to invest in their e-commerce operations. We hired people who had been laid off and had expertise in this area, and started building out a new practice to replace the one we had lost. By the time normality returned, and with it our branding work, we had a whole new arm of the business, one that had been grown out of necessity but made us stronger and more diversified for the long term. In the process, though I didn't realize at the time, we'd also developed a de facto crisis playbook that would prove very useful when the banks went under in 2007–8, taking much of our business with them.

The pivot may be forced on you, as it was on bars and restaurants during Covid, many of which turned instead to delivery and food-to-go services. But in many cases, the path won't be so obvious. The warning signs won't be so loud and you may be tempted to ignore them. You may convince yourself that you will be fine if you carry on largely as you are. "That interesting technology others are investing in sounds quite expensive." "That emerging trend sounds like a fad." "Those new competitors won't last the course." That is not persistence but stagnation. It is the kind of complacency that leads businesses into the graveyard.

That's why I say that to persist you must also pivot and know when to take your business in new directions, whether that is towards a new opportunity or away from a gathering threat. Persistence is about survival, and survivors in business are those that constantly adapt and evolve in a dynamic world that never slows down so that you can catch up.

By contrast, businesses that fail are so often ones that didn't persist when persistence was needed most. If I mention Blockbuster, the once-dominant movie rental company, you will probably recall that they failed because of the rise of Netflix. You may even know the story of how they once turned down the chance to *buy* Netflix—often described as one of the worst business decisions ever made.

Because of this, most people think their failure was due to a lack of innovation and foresight. A more nimble competitor with a clearer view of the future ate their lunch. But that wasn't quite how it happened. In reality, Blockbuster fought back well against the threat of Netflix in the mid 2000s. It built its own online subscription service, which grew just as rapidly as its younger rival. One of Netflix's cofounders later recalled that they were seriously worried that Blockbuster, which could leverage not just an online operation but its vast network of retail stores, would squash them.[3] That might have happened, and the history of the streaming business might have been very different. But then Blockbuster ran into trouble: it had a significant amount of debt, its major shareholders disagreed on what direction to go in, and they ended up firing the CEO who had led the charge against Netflix, after which the subscription service withered and the company went bankrupt within a few years. Blockbuster didn't lose because it failed to see the future or tried to ignore it. It lost because of a lack of persistence. The complications in and around its business meant it gave up on a potentially winning strategy too early. It didn't stay the course and the business didn't survive.

That is why persistence matters. Without it, you are certain to fail before long. Whereas if you carry on until you get lucky, learn to thrive in adversity, and accept the necessity of ripping up the script at regular intervals, then there is every chance that your business will prosper over the long term.

And as it does, you may start to wonder: what comes next? Do I still want to be running this company after five, ten, or fifteen years? Is it still the most rewarding way I can be spending my time, and the best available means of pursuing my dream? Now that we are reaching the end of this journey, we need to consider what a good finale (and the new beginning that follows) will look like. We need to look at how to develop your role over time, if and how to sell your business, and how to work out what happens after. Every business has a natural lifespan, and so too does the place of a founder within that business. You need to think about and plan for the ending as carefully as you did the beginning.

13

Sell and Start Again

Never quit. Never give up. Always keep going.

It's advice you hear a lot in the business world. After a whole chapter where I have talked about the importance of persistence, you probably think I agree with it. But I don't.

I prefer the wisdom of the Kenny Rogers song, "The Gambler," which tells us there is a time to keep going, and a time to quit.

Every business and every business journey has a natural life. You might run that business for just six months or a year, because it's teaching you how to do it and letting you make all your mistakes in one go (for me that was the gardening company I started aged fifteen). Or you might have run the business for twenty years and be ready to sell for a major payday that will change your life. Or, after whatever length of time, your role might have changed to the point where it is natural you will hand over the business to your management team and focus on your other commitments.

Regardless, the truth is that **there will come a time when quitting is the right decision** for you. You walk away either because the money is too good to turn down, you want to be spending your time on something else, or simply because you are burned out and not having fun anymore. In the right circumstances, quitting rocks. It really does.

That is different from what I talked about in the last chapter, when I said that you can't give up when things get difficult. That is true when you are in the middle of the journey: when the business is at a critical moment, and you are fighting to survive. Quitting then is giving up. Whereas leaving at the right time, when you have reached the end of the road, is just common sense. If quitting means giving up on your dream, then you are doing it at the wrong time; but if walking away will allow you to keep on pursuing that dream in a new or better way, then it's probably the right one.

That's a lesson it took me a long time to learn, and which I needed my life partner to teach me. I've never forgotten the day Helen suddenly turned around and told me she wanted to leave Fluid. We had been so focused on building the business together, working hand in hand for a full ten years, that it had never occurred to me that we wouldn't carry on together until the finish line. I was completely blindsided when Helen told me she'd had enough and wanted to step down: she was such an intrinsic part of the business that I couldn't imagine it without her. Like a little boy, the first word out of my mouth was simply "Why?"

I'm ashamed to admit that my first reaction to Helen's decision was selfish. I thought most about how terrible it was for me and how hard it was going to be to run the company without my life and business partner. Only when the shock had worn off, and I remembered that my wife is an infinitely wiser person than I am, did I start to see it from her perspective. Helen had started Fluid with me while in her early twenties. In career terms, graphic design had been all she'd known. Now she was at a different stage in her life, she had fallen out of love with the work, and she saw there could be more. Specifically, she wanted to become a kinesiologist, specializing in a form of natural holistic therapy that supports physical, emotional, and mental health, something that would take years of training. The sooner she started on that path, the better.

At first, Helen's decision stunned me. But soon I began to respect the strength of character and self-awareness it had taken to realize that she was done with this stage of her life, and then to act on it. What's more, some time had passed, I began to realize that I felt the same way. As is the case for a lot of entrepreneurs, the passion I'd had in the early years of running my business had started to ebb away. I felt like I had seen it all, was learning nothing new, and was at risk of being stuck on a treadmill where I was doing the same things over and over.

While I was getting bored of the marketing services world, I was also starting to get interested in other things and had become involved in Hong Kong's budding start-up scene. I wanted to help entrepreneurs and invest in companies, rather than continuing to devote my entire focus to a single business. If I'd known about my dream at that point (which I didn't), I would have realized that it was evolving and I had reached the point where I needed a new outlet for it.

I had reached the classic entrepreneur's midlife crisis. I was closer to the end of my time with the business than the beginning, but at that point I didn't know when and how I would exit. I wasn't sure of which steps to take, and in what order.

In the three years between Helen leaving the business and us selling it, I did some things right and others wrong. We got to the right ending but not necessarily in the most efficient way. With the benefit of that experience, I want to finish by showing you what to do when you are reaching the end of a business journey. How do you divorce your own company? When and how should you sell? And how, after you have done that, do you keep the dream alive?

How to divorce your business

Any entrepreneur will tell you that it hurts to let go. However big or small, famous or unknown it is, the business you created is your baby. You gave it life and nurtured it. You saw it grow and overcome challenges. For a time, possibly quite a long time, that business was your life. You spent almost all your waking hours working on it, and you answered its needs before any others. You took personally every failure and setback and did everything in your power to try to overcome them.

There's a reason that a lot of famous founders ended up going back to the businesses they started. Steve Jobs returned to save Apple, Howard Schultz made not one but two comebacks at Starbucks, and Jack Dorsey had a second go at running Twitter. When Alphabet (Google's parent company) was seen to be falling behind in the AI race after the launch of ChatGPT (in which Microsoft was an investor), it was reported that cofounders Larry Page and Sergey Brin became more directly involved in the business than they had been for years.

It sums up how hard it is for an entrepreneur to step back from the business they created. Because giving up control—in theory—is one thing. Actually accepting that the business is no longer yours, and acting like it, is another. This is where things get difficult, no matter whether you are Mark Zuckerberg or someone running a small gardening business. That's why you need to understand what it means to divorce your business and how to do it well.

The first thing about divorcing well is doing it at the right time. I knew it was time for me, a few years after Helen had come to that decision for herself, because my mind was increasingly on other things. Remember how I said that you will know your dream is real because you won't be able to stop yourself from thinking about it? After a little over a decade running Fluid, that wasn't happening anymore. I saw new business pitches as a chore rather than something exciting and nerve-racking. I had no motivation to sit down and write a new list of fifty great clients I wanted to go out and win. The fire in me to run that business was flickering low. I was ready for the separation.

I can't exactly tell you how this feels, but I'm pretty sure you will know. Subconsciously, your body and brain are crying out for something different. It might take a bit of time to admit it to yourself, but you are done. You have to know and recognize the signs of dwindling passion and motivation. You will get those things back when you start again and find a new vehicle for your dream but, as far as this business goes, you are in the end game and you shouldn't try to hide from it.

By the same token, you can't allow yourself to be talked into leaving your business before you are ready. There are people who will sing you a siren song—it's a good time to sell; it would be a lot easier if you got in a professional manager to run the shop; you can still hold on to the equity and have an easier life. If someone is talking you into quitting your business, then don't listen. If you follow their advice, I can almost guarantee you will end up either regretting the decision or trying to re-verse it by taking the business over again. Don't get divorced when there is still love in the marriage.

But if you are ready to move on, then you need to plan for it. Unless something has gone badly wrong, leaving the business you started is not a sudden process. Whether you are going to maintain an ownership stake or sell up entirely, you need to exit in the way that will be best for both you and the business. Unless you are winding it down, then you want to ensure stability for the people working in the business, as well as maximizing its value as an asset (for their and your good, since if you have followed my advice, you will have given your employees equity).

Trying to quit your business in one go is a bit like trying to kick a nicotine addiction overnight. It's far better to taper off gradually, reducing your role until the whole thing runs without you. My advice is to move in stages. Give away one part of your day job, pick a person to run it, help them get up to speed, and then leave them alone. Then do it again. Keep doing it until you are nothing more than a figurehead who can be called on if necessary, but is no longer relied upon. At that point you are divorced: you can either sell your stake and cut ties entirely, or remain an owner but retreat into an arm's-length role where you may do little more than act as an ambassador and attend a few board meetings every year. If you are staying involved, try to err on the side of doing less rather than more. It's not your show anymore, and you have to know when it's time to get off the stage.

That is basically how things went with Fluid, though in retrospect I made a number of mistakes on the way. I held on to too much responsibility for too long, and when I did decide that I needed to replace myself, I initially picked someone for the wrong reasons: not because they had the experience and knowledge to run a business like this, but because I knew and liked them. For longer than I should have, I stuck by this person and kept insisting that I could help them get up to speed despite mounting evidence to the contrary.

In the end, family reasons meant that they had to leave Hong Kong, and I got a second chance at replacing myself. This time I set myself a very clear brief: I wanted someone who was in a senior management position in another agency, but who had little or no ownership stake (which is what I was offering). I wanted a top professional with a track record who could not just do the job I had, but do it better and take the business to the next level. I identified and met eight people. After having coffee with all of them, I came to a realization: any single one of them would do a better job of running Fluid now than I could. I picked the best person, they went on to do exactly that, and within two years we had sold the business for more than I had ever expected.

That experience taught me the final lesson about how to get divorced from the company you founded. You have to leave your ego behind. A bit of ego probably helped in building the business: when you have almost nothing, you need to tell yourself that you are great, you will make the sale, and you can achieve your dream. But when you are running a mature business, ego gets in the way and starts to undermine you. Instead, remember the three T's: train people, trust people, and tear yourself away. Step back and learn to accept a different role. Admire the view of what you have built from a distance. And if your ego is feeling at all bruised, then comfort yourself with this fact: by having effectively fired yourself, you have made it a lot easier to take the next step and sell your company.

How to sell your business

Stepping away from the business in the right way and at the right time is all well and good. But I can almost hear you saying: come on, how do I sell the damn thing?

Well, there's a very simple rule for selling a business and it's this: don't try to sell your business. I am not trying to be funny or clever here. But if you stick up the equivalent of a "for sale" sign in front of your office, then the price immediately goes down. You have put yourself at a disadvantage. Everyone knows you are for sale, and you don't have to be a business expert to know that you can get a good price when you buy from a motivated seller.

The truly valuable things in life are the ones we want but think we can't have. That's what your business needs to be if you are going to sell it well: a prize asset that potential purchasers think may be out of their reach. Rather than being a motivated seller, you have to create motivated buyers.

How, then, do you sell a business without looking as if you are trying to sell it?

The simple answer is that you get to know the people who might buy your business, build relationships with them, strike up partnerships where relevant, and then wait to see what happens.

At Fluid I had a pretty clear idea of how the endgame for the business would look. Long before I had hired someone to take over as CEO in preparation for a sale, I knew who I thought would be the eventual buyer for our company. It was one of the big, global advertising firms with a presence in Hong Kong. Sometimes they were our competitor and at other points our partner on projects, but as time went on I tried to make the relationship more and more friendly. I pushed the partnership angle and built relationships with their main executives. I thought that if we were going to sell Fluid to anyone, it would be these guys.

I was dead wrong. That deal never came close to happening. And when a deal did happen, it took me completely by surprise. I would never have believed that we would end up selling to PricewaterhouseCoopers (PwC), a consulting firm with its roots in accountancy. But PwC, like a lot of the big consultancies, was increasingly dipping its toe into selling creative services. They had engaged us to work on several projects with them. As we did more together, they soon decided it would be easier just to buy Fluid and make it part of their own team.

That is why I say you shouldn't go looking for a buyer for your company. If you focus on growing the business and networking within and outside your industry, you may be surprised who comes shopping for you. Make yourself visible without making a point of saying that you are up for sale. Trust that people have eyes and can see that your business is doing something innovative or different that is driving its success. Focus on being so good that the competition cannot ignore you, or beat you, so they have no option but to try to buy you.

Even then, pause and be sure about what you are doing. The fact that someone has put an offer on the table doesn't mean you have to sell. And you should only sell if that offer meets certain criteria: if it's good for you, because you have decided to move on and this gives you the liquidity and the opportunity to do so; if it's good for the people in the business, who you persuaded to join you on this journey; and if it's good for the business itself, and you believe you will be leaving the brand you so lovingly created in safe hands.

PwC was not the first company that tried to buy Fluid, and theirs was not the biggest offer we received. But I knew it was the right offer, because we had worked with them, they respected our purpose to elevate creativity and creative people, and because they made a commitment that they would increase the salaries of all our people on day one of their ownership. It was a deal that was good for the majority shareholders of Fluid and good for everyone who wanted to carry on working in the business. It was a no-brainer.

Later, I sold my investment company, Nest, in a different

way. That was a management buyout, where the chief executive put together a deal to take it over. Essentially, you are bought out of your own company by the management team (or in this case one of them), which can be a good way of exiting if the other people want to carry on running the business without new ownership, and can raise the necessary funding to purchase your equity.

However you go about trying to sell your business, my advice is to be certain that you want to. Although it was undoubtedly the right thing to do at the time, I sometimes regret that I sold Fluid. I now know that it has taken three or four years to get back to the point where I have an operation and a team with which I can do the work I am interested in. In another world, I would have retained ownership of Fluid and used the business as a platform to do everything I am doing now through HelpBnk.

But in the world we have, I did sell my business and was then left with the question that any exited entrepreneur faces: what next? What happens when you have scaled one mountain and been very well rewarded for your efforts? How do you start again and keep on chasing the dream?

How to start again

The very first business I sold did not make me very much money, but it did teach me an important lesson. I'd started it when I was working on a hotel reception desk, the last job I did in the UK before moving to Hong Kong. It wasn't long before it became clear that we were sitting on a missed opportunity. This was 1996, and when the hotel was fully booked, we would tell people who called up asking for a room that we couldn't help them. One night, because I wanted to help someone who sounded in need, I rang up another hotel and arranged for them to provide a room. Soon, working with the other receptionists, this had grown into a business: we diverted all the excess traffic coming through our switchboard to hotels with available rooms, and received commission in return. We called it Accommodation Express.

This was Booking.com before the internet had become mainstream, but I didn't have the confidence or motivation at that point in my life to scale it. In the end, I sold the business for not very much, and it was at that point I learned what happens next.

When you have made money as an entrepreneur, even a small amount, suddenly people line up to tell you what to do with it. Put the money into a house, they will say. Invest in the stock market. Use it to generate passive income. A lot of people who have never started or run a business themselves are very confident about telling people who have how they should spend the money they have made.

My advice is: don't listen to any of this. Don't get sucked in by the finance industry telling you that they know best what to do with your money. Don't listen to the people who tell you how great it will be to retire early (I think retirement is for people who hate what they do). And don't accept the narrative that your best and most important work is now behind you. A great example is Tony Fadell, an entrepreneur I interviewed on my podcast. As an employee at Apple, he became known as the "father of the iPod" for his work leading the team that developed this iconic product. He also went on to play a critical role in the creation of the iPhone. After that, a lot of people would have decided to bank their winnings and go to the beach. Instead, he left Apple, started his own company based around smart home devices, Nest Labs, and within four years had sold that business to Google for $3.2 billion.

So remember that the best is almost always still to come. But that doesn't mean you have to rush it, and you should also be easy on yourself. When you have spent years focusing on one thing, it can take a while to shake off the tunnel vision and start thinking about your life in broader terms. You might not know immediately what the next business, project, or campaign is going to be. You might want to take some time just to enjoy yourself, which is fine as long as you accept that it shouldn't be forever, and you will soon get bored of golf and the beach.

The question of how to start again is going to depend on what stage you have reached in your life and career. If you are young and made some money from a business, but not enough that you never have to worry about money again, then the answer is pretty simple. You have to invest in yourself. Find the next business: the one that was too expensive or complicated the first time, but for which you now have the capital or experience. Tackle the big project that has been lurking at the back of your mind. Swing big, because now you have the means, the experience, and probably the contacts to do it. Go back to your dream and your purpose and ask yourself: what is the biggest and best articulation of this? What is the most ambitious version?

Also, if you have not done so before, *travel*. Going to Hong Kong at the age of twenty-three changed my life. It may sound cheesy, but it really did help me to see the world differently and to understand that the place I had grown up in was just one bubble among millions. I promise that seeing more of the world, different people and cultures will change the way you build businesses: you will understand that the market is so much bigger and more varied, and the opportunity so much vaster than you had realized.

If you are not so young, or you've made a truly life-changing amount of money, then it may be more complicated. The lure of the beach will be that much stronger. But here is the thing: your dream has not gone away. If you were ambitious and driven enough to build a successful business, you are unlikely to be the kind of person who is satisfied with selling it and strolling into the sunset. You know you are still young enough and you still have a contribution to make. You can make a difference in whatever your field may be. Perhaps you will go the whole hog and start another business from the beginning, or you may prefer to become an investor, mentor, or adviser to other entrepreneurs. You might want to pursue the same purpose that drove your initial business but through a not-for-profit or social impact vehicle, which you are now capable of funding.

If you have started this journey from the beginning, building a business based on a dream, then you will probably know which direction to go in next. You have your compass points. If, like me, you only worked out midway through that you'd had a dream all along, then you may need to recalibrate. What I worked out after selling up was that I had been motivated all along by an interest in helping people with their businesses: with Fluid I had done this in return for fees, and at Nest in return for equity. Now I had the means to start doing it for free: that was the basis for HelpBnk and everything that has come with it.

That is the thing about dreams, and why they have been the basis for this book. You can sell your business, but no one can ever buy your dream off you. The dream persists and remains as important as it ever was. And if you have made money, then you are in a better position than ever to be ambitious in how you pursue your dream. The dream can be bigger and better than before. One restaurant in your home town might grow into a group that spans the world. The mission behind your successful business could become the focal point of a wider campaign which you run or fund. Your career as a filmmaker, architect, or writer might evolve into helping others achieve the same dream.

That's why I think that, even turning fifty and with over three decades of my career behind me, I am only halfway done with my dream. I am helping people for free, HelpBnk is growing and our ideas are spreading, but there is so much more to do. I am still motivated by the memory of being homeless at fifteen, desperately needing help, and not being able to get it. I want to create something where people can click a button and get the help they need in a meaningful way, because so many people have united around our purpose and #GiveWithoutTake philosophy that we are able to provide it.

That may sound like pie in the sky to you, but that is the point of an ambitious dream. It's an aspiration so big and a destination so distant that you have to keep going, finding new ways to unlock it and go further towards it. It's the antidote to complacency, cynicism, and the thought that the world is too big and complicated for us to make a difference. I will not stop with my work until there isn't a person who could benefit from my help who isn't getting it. Which in reality means I will carry on until I drop, and then other people can pick up the baton and adopt the mission.

That is why I have spent so much of this book talking about the importance of the dream and the necessity of asking yourself the really fundamental questions: what do I like doing; what is my purpose; what does success look like for me; what's my dream? If you can work out the answers to those questions, as early as possible, then you are doing the most important thing you can to set yourself up for success. You are putting a deep sense of meaning at the heart of everything you do.

And while so many things in life change, these do not. True, they may evolve: your dream may take on new dimensions, your purpose may expand, you may think differently about success as you travel through life. But the fundamentals of these things will remain constant. The things that really matter to us will go on being important no matter what else changes. The dream will stay with you, and you will find new outlets for it as your life progresses.

The alternative is that you live according to other people's needs and priorities: that you change jobs because a recruiter rang you up trying to get a commission; that you keep climbing the career "ladder" because you are influenced by other people's idea of success; and that you avoid taking risks because you fear failure more than you embrace the possibility of success.

Abandoning all that and living life on your own terms is one of the most liberating and powerful choices you can make. You will be amazed how clearly you see when you stop trying to please people who aren't important, or live up to some standardized vision of what your life should be.

If you take one message away from the book, I hope it's this. **Set your own goals, judge your own success, and be accountable to yourself and the people you care about. Do something you love and can be brilliant at. Have a dream and pursue a purpose.** Hold on to these things and they will be the best investment you ever make. I can't promise it will be easy. But you can overcome more pain and adversity than you believed possible when you know you are doing the right thing, and moving in the right direction. In search of what matters. Towards the dream.

Afterword

#TakeFour

This book has been about how to change your life by discovering and pursuing your dream. That's a long-term project and, as I have said several times, it will involve plenty of delayed gratification.

But not everything has to be about the far-distant future. There are things you can and should do today—right now—that will put you on the path towards that future. I want to end this book by sharing the most important one with you.

I call it #TakeFour. It's incredibly simple.

Starting today, take four minutes out of your day. Find a way to help someone, ideally a stranger.

Take one minute to find out who they are.

One minute to find out what they need.

One minute to give them some help.

One minute to pass it on so that someone else can do the same.

It's only four minutes, so it won't be anything very big or complicated. Maybe you stop on the street to ask someone raising money what it's about. Maybe you pause to answer someone's question on LinkedIn because you have an insight to share or a contact who could help. Perhaps you share the story of someone who inspired you on social media, post a positive review of a small business you had a good experience with, or stop to talk to someone who is homeless outside a supermarket, hear their story, and offer to buy them some food.

Why are these simple actions so important? It's because we live in a world that, like it or not, is increasingly built around and optimized for technology. Whether you are doing your weekly shop or trying to find love, we are encouraged to swipe and click where we once spoke to a person.

Now I am not a luddite. I love technology and have built multiple businesses around it. But even people who enjoy our tech-centric world need to acknowledge that there is a price to pay for all this convenience. Digital enablers may have made our world more efficient in many ways, but they've also made it increasingly transactional and impersonal. We expect things to happen quickly and we get frustrated if they don't. And because we are interacting more with machines than people, we end up having fewer random and unplanned conversations. We find out less about other people, and our lives become a little smaller and less interesting as a result.

That is the purpose of #TakeFour. It's about connecting back to people, especially those we don't already know. It's about being more curious about the world, hearing more stories, and having more chance encounters.

Above all, it's about **giving help and expecting nothing in return**. It's #GiveWithoutTake in action. Why does that matter? Because every time someone has to pay or work hard to get help, it stops them from helping the next person. But if you give them the help freely, they are liberated to do the same. One interaction at a time, we can flip a transactional world of "give and take" into one where people want to help others, and are empowered to do so.

That is what I am trying to achieve with everything I do. I think most people *want* to help others, but the world is increasingly designed to get in the way of this. Technology entrenches the transactional mindset. You get my data and I get something for free. I pay and you boost my profile to potential matches. I sign up to your newsletter so you give me a discount.

I want people to break free of these transactions and just embrace the act of helping. One person helps another, who helps a third. A chain reaction, in which your simple act of #GiveWithoutTake ultimately impacts someone you will never meet.

That may sound altruistic, but what's good for the world is also good for you. Helping someone every day is going to help you and support you on the journey I have set out in this book. Because when you help someone, it changes you. It awakens something: not just the feeling we get when we put a smile on someone's face, but a confidence that you can make a difference and an awareness about how to do it.

Remember that in working out what your dream is, the third step after asking what you like doing and what pain is motivating you is to define how you can help people: how to make your passion and purpose in life intersect with the world around you. Well, let me shock you by telling you that the best way of working out how you can help people is to help people. I truly believe that in order to make your dream come true, you need to help someone else's dream come true. Give it a go: it's worth a try, isn't it, and what's the downside if I am wrong?

That is my final challenge to you. Help someone out today, and do it again tomorrow, and again the day after. Listen to someone else's dream and do one tiny thing to help them make it happen. Give for the sake of giving, and expect nothing in return. I guarantee that, in doing so, you will have taken another step towards your own dream. So go on. #TakeFour. Post about it. Tag me in. Let's continue the conversation and see how far it can go.

Acknowledgments

Most of all, I want to thank Helen Griffiths for partnering up with me twenty-four years ago to start a business that changed both our lives, and for being the best wife and mother in the world.

Thank you to my older brother, Christian, for showing me the world and my potential.

To the Brennan family, for helping me when I was down and being there to show me what a loving family looks like.

My partners at HelpBnk, for joining me and putting their energy into building something with the same love and care as I have for it. I know we are not meant to say it, but they are not just colleagues: to me, they are friends. AJ, Adam, Adrien, Ben, Chloe, Callum, Dudley, James, Jack, Jess, Yordi, Samir, Phebe, Will, and Joe—together we will help millions help millions.

Josh Davis, who helped me take the ideas in my head and write them down.

Lawrence Morgan and Guy Parsonage for helping make Fluid work.

Callum Crute and the team at Century, and Adam Gauntlett, for believing in the dream that was this book and making it happen.

I want to thank you, the readers, for following me online and helping make dreams happen, and for reading this book and helping me pass on the message that it's time to #GiveWithoutTake.

Acknowledgments

After thirty-five years in business, the full list of people who have helped me could be a book in itself.

My final thanks are to all those who have supported me through this journey, who are too numerous to mention by name, but without whom this book could never have been written and the lessons it never learned.

Notes

1.
The Myths About Life

1   V. Chow, "HK comic makes foray into Hollywood, with US$80m adaptation on the cards," *South China Morning Post*, August 8, 2009.

2.
Why a Dream Matters

1   C. Gardner, *The Pursuit of Happyness*, Amistad, 2006.

2   M. Yousafzai and P. McCormick, *I Am Malala: How One Girl Stood Up for Education and Changed the World*, Little, Brown, 2016.

3   Stallone quotes via "The Greatest Underdog Story Ever Told: Stallone on Making Rocky," Jer Films, youtube.com.

3.
Why Purpose Matters

1   M. Makara-Studzinska, Z. Wajda, S. Lizinczyk, "Years of service, self-efficacy, stress and burnout among Polish

firefighters," *International Journal of Occupational Medicine and Environmental Health*, 2020, 33(3):283–297; G. Crea, L. Francis, "Purpose in Life as Protection Against Professional Burnout Among Catholic Priests and Religious in Italy: Testing the Insights of Logotherapy," *Pastoral Psychology*, 2022, 71:471–483.

2 J. McKoy, "Higher sense of purpose in life may be linked to lower mortality risk, study finds," *Science Daily*, November 15, 2022, via www.sciencedaily.com.

3 E. Kim, V. Strecher, C. Ryff, "Purpose in life and use of preventive health care services," *Proceedings of the National Academy of Sciences*, 2014, 111(46):16331–16336.

4 A. Van Dam, "The happiest, least stressful, most meaningful jobs in America," *Washington Post*, January 6, 2023.

6.
Free Yourself

1 A. Wilkins, "Will Amazon's robotic revolution spark a new wave of job losses?" *New Scientist*, April 23, 2024.

12.
Keep Going

1 S. Witt, "How Jensen Huang's Nvidia Is Powering the AI Revolution," *The New Yorker*, November 27, 2023.

Notes

2 "Nvidia CEO Jensen Huang on Building Resilience with Pain and Suffering," PodiumVC, youtube.com.

3 T. Huddlestone Jr., "Netflix didn't kill Blockbuster—how Netflix almost lost the movie rental wars," CNBC, September 22, 2020, via www.cnbc.com.

About the Author

Simon Squibb, founder of HelpBnk, is all about helping people help people. Not your typical entrepreneur, Simon started his first business while homeless at just fifteen and later sold his agency, Fluid, to PwC for more money than he'll ever need. Known for his viral move of buying a staircase in London and slapping a doorbell on it where folks can pitch their dreams, Simon is on a mission to help ten million people kick-start their businesses. With over ten million followers on social media, he's spreading the word through his #GiveWithoutTake movement and inspirational street interviews.